OPERATING
IN THE
MIRACULOUS

STEVE HILL

Clarion Call Marketing

OPERATING IN THE MIRACULOUS

Published by:
Clarion Call Marketing, Inc.
Dallas, Texas

Copyright © 2005 Clarion Call Marketing, Inc.

ISBN: 1-59574-013-9

Printed in the United States of America.

08 07 06 05   1 2 3 4 5 6

OPERATING
IN THE
MIRACULOUS

TABLE OF CONTENTS

*To my mom, Ann Hill, who recently laid down her torch
and went on to be with the Lord. This woman of faith knew how
to get hold of God and believe Him for the miraculous.*

*And to you, the reader, who will be challenged
to pick up the torch, burn brightly for Jesus,
believe God with increasing faith,
and begin operating in the miraculous.*

INTRODUCTION

You Can Operate in the Miraculous

MY WHOLE CHRISTIAN LIFE has been filled with miracles. In fact, my Christian walk began with a miracle.

When I was twenty-one, I had already been a drug addict for many years. I had started drinking alcohol at age ten and first tried drugs at age twelve. By twenty-one, the lights were going out inside Steve Hill, the final curtain was coming down. I was dying, and I knew it. Twisted with convulsions, every nerve ending on fire with agonizing pain, I was terrified of dying but knew there was nothing I could do to save myself.

In an instant, our miracle-working God healed my body and set me free from bondage to drugs and alcohol. You'll read about the mind-blowing details of that miracle later in this book. For now, be assured that I know a miracle when I see—or experience—one.

My wife's salvation story is another miracle I will share later, along with the stunning reports of the many miracles Jeri and I have witnessed over the years. We have seen thousands upon thousands of people saved, healed, and delivered by the power of God in our meetings. I myself have been cured from an *incurable* disease. During the Argentine Revival and the Brownsville Revival in Pensacola—both of

> *God wants to take natural people and work supernaturally through them to bring about a mighty surge of His power.... I challenge you to make yourself ready for Him to use you in this wonderful moment in which we live today.*
> —LESTER SUMRALL (1913-1996)[1]

which we were privileged to be part of—we observed firsthand the awesome, miracle-working power of God on an almost daily basis. The Bible proclaims and our personal experience bears out that God *wants* to work miracles on behalf of His children, and it probably puzzles Him that more of us aren't asking Him to act in miraculous ways on our behalf.

Jesus thought nothing of asking God for a miracle. After all, He was with God and He was God when the walls of Jericho crumbled, when the Red Sea parted, when the sun stood still, when Jonah survived three days in the belly of the great fish. He knew from experience that His Father is all powerful and that the Father's power is His also.

Amazingly, the Old Testament saints, who did not have the example of Jesus to follow, were also bold in asking for miracles. Elijah prophesied an unending supply of meal and oil to feed himself and the household of the widow who took him in in the city of Zarephath. Later, he even raised her son from the dead. Elijah's servant Elisha had a gift of healing and cleansed Naaman the leper. The New Testament, of course, is full of miracles, as the followers of Jesus learned to rely upon the power of the Holy Spirit. So why now, when there are more Christians on the face of the earth than at any other time in history, have so many Christians become reluctant to ask and believe for a miracle?

Perhaps we have forgotten that God has a greater design for our lives—a purpose and plan for my life and for your life and for every believer...and His plan is *not* for us to live with some low-level, powerless, defeatism mentality. He does not want us to look back with longing on the miracles of the past as if they were for a certain time and season but are no longer available to us. He does not want us to feel that our prayers accomplish nothing, that our faith *can't* move mountains, that we lack the strength to make a difference.

All of that is utterly untrue, and yet it is the attitude you see in many mainstream churches. They don't expect miracles because they feel powerless. If a miracle happens right in front of them, they look for the catch or for the smoke and mirrors. Because they do not believe they serve a God of miracles, they do not pursue His power, which is readily available.

If you doubt the static state of many mainstream churches in America, look no further than the surveys which find that rates of divorce, depression, and alcoholism are about the same for those who attend church as for those who don't. It is obvious that many churches are not helping their members experience God to the full, "having a form of godliness but denying its power" (2 Timothy 3:5).

God's plan for you is the direct opposite of that travesty. He has called you to be victorious! He has called you to be more than a conqueror (Romans 8:37). Why come to Christ if not to be filled with His power to be useful to His kingdom?

Why struggle along in a lackluster spiritual walk when Jesus has told you, "All authority has been given to Me in heaven and on earth. Go therefore and make disciples of all the nations, baptizing them in the name of the Father and of the Son and of the Holy Spirit" (Matthew 28:18-19), and "He who believes in Me, the works that I do he will do also; and greater works than these he will do, because I go to My Father. And whatever you ask in My name, that I will do, that the Father may be glorified in the Son" (John 14:12-13).

In these passages Jesus conferred His authority upon you to do the same works (healing, casting out demons, raising the dead) and even greater works than these. With this as our Gospel heritage, why are we not living up to it? Why aren't we walking in it daily?

Perhaps you feel that you cannot do what Jesus has promised you can do because you aren't Jesus. Why should He expect you to do miracles? Actually, He expects you to do them because He said so, just as He did miracles because His Father said so. When Jesus came to earth as a man, He laid down His divine powers.

He said: "I say to you, the Son can do nothing of Himself, but what He sees the Father do; for whatever He does, the Son also does in like manner" (John 5:19) and "I can of Myself do nothing…because I do not seek My own will but the will of the Father who sent Me" (John 5:30) and "I do nothing of Myself; but as My Father taught Me, I speak these things" (John 8:28).

How much more clearly could Jesus spell out for us that He did miracles on earth, *not* because He was God incarnate with divine power, but because He was relying totally on God to work through Him by the Holy Spirit? This is what He wants us to do as well. "For I have given you an example, that you should do as I have done to you" (John 13:15).

The Scripture is full of promises and commands for *all* believers to operate in the miraculous:

> And as you go, preach, saying, "The kingdom of heaven is at hand." Heal the sick, cleanse the lepers, raise the dead, cast out demons. Freely you have received, freely give. (Matthew 10:7-8)

> Then He called His twelve disciples together and gave them power and authority over all demons, and to cure diseases. He sent them to preach the kingdom of God and to heal the sick. (Luke 9:1-2)

> But you shall receive power when the Holy Spirit has come upon you; and you shall be witnesses to Me in Jerusalem, and in all Judea and Samaria, and to the end of the earth. (Acts 1:8)

> Now this is the confidence that we have in Him, that if we ask anything according to His will, He hears us. And if we know that He hears us, whatever we ask, we know that we have the petitions that we have asked of Him. (1 John 5:14-15)

These promises and commands are for you and me. God wants *us* to lay hands on our sick family members and see them recover. God wants *us* to lay hold of His promises for provision to obtain financial breakthrough. God wants *us* to be able to minister His delivering power when a loved one is tormented by the enemy.

What I have seen and experienced over the past three decades has convinced me of this one thing: we *desperately* need God's power in our lives, our homes, and our churches more than ever before. And He is more than willing to pour that power into us!

Keep in mind, this power already belongs to Jesus, and He has already conveyed it to us, His joint heirs. And this authority isn't about meeting only your personal needs. God's plan extends far beyond that.

As a believer, you are on the most serious mission on earth. You are called to be a light in the darkness. You have been given a mandate to sow the seed of His Word into the hearts of mankind. Jesus has commissioned you and me to go into all the world and preach the Gospel to every creature (Mark 16:15). This is called the Great Commission, not the Great Consideration. You don't have the option of deciding whether or not to fulfill it.

To *every* Christian, Christ has given the command to go and preach the Gospel, and then some. Tacked on to that order to preach is an element that shakes some Christians to the core. Though totally ignored by some, it fills others, like you and me, with great joy and anticipation.

Immediately after the Great Commission, Jesus said, "And these signs will follow those who believe: In My name they will cast out demons; they will speak with new tongues; they will take up serpents; and if they drink anything deadly, it will by no means hurt them; they will lay hands on the sick, and they will recover" (Mark 16:17-18). There it is. We are to cast out demons, lay hands on the sick, and they will recover.

Simply put, Jesus has chosen you and me as vessels to manifest His power. From *us* is to flow, not only hope for the hopeless and love for the unloved, but also healing virtue for those who are sick and delivering power for those who are bound.

This is the message of this book: Ordinary believers like you and me have the potential in Christ to accomplish extraordinary things—even miraculous things—for the kingdom of heaven. In fact, we not only have the potential to do so, but we have been commanded to do so. And God would not command us to do something that He in His awesome power was not going to make possible.

This book is not an exhaustive study of miracles, although you will see plenty from the Scriptures and read examples of modern-day miracles and their purposes. Although I thank God for them, this book is not a history of the great ministers of the past and present who have operated and are operating in the miraculous. This book is designed only to launch you on a spiritual journey that culminates in your flowing in the power of God, every day of your life, with signs and wonders manifested through your personal ministry.

You don't have to be a pastor, evangelist, teacher, or minister to learn from this book or to manifest God's power. Jesus didn't leave His authority only with ordained ministers—He left it with each believer.

When I first began this teaching with a small-group study guide for my church, Heartland Fellowship Church in Dallas/Fort Worth, dozens of Bible study groups met each week, not at church to hear a preacher, but in individual homes to study God's Word, discuss His power, and develop their faith for the miraculous. These groups began to see miracles manifested, not through me, not through a teacher on the church staff, but through these individual laypeople who had discovered God's power to operate in the miraculous.

I think of Jeanne, a member of our church who had an unsaved friend in the hospital dying of cancer. At the time, I was preaching the message "Operating in the Miraculous" at Heartland. Jeanne was especially burdened for her friend because she was so close to slipping into eternity without Christ. On the way to the hospital she prayed, "Lord, give me a window of opportunity." When she arrived at the hospital, her friend was in a comatose state. Jeanne had just heard me preach on the importance of building an atmosphere for a miracle, so she did something she had never done before. She prayed for her friend and then began to sing songs of healing. The whole atmosphere in the room changed. As a result, Jeanne's friend came out of the coma, and Jeanne led her to Christ.

I believe that when the Christ-honoring Christians in the pews take up this calling we will begin to see the greatest days of harvest the church has ever experienced. And the only way we can see that massive harvest is by the power of God. That's what I want to pour into you through the study of this book and God's Word. I am thrilled to share with you the message God has given me about operating in the miraculous. As you receive these truths, you will be prepared for God to use you in ways you never dreamed possible. Yes, you can operate in the miraculous! It can happen to you!

Steve Hill
Senior Pastor
Heartland Fellowship Church
Dallas/Fort Worth, Texas

EVERYDAY MIRACLES

WHAT IS A MIRACLE? You hear different definitions and usages of the word: "It will be a miracle if we can pay our bills this month!" or "I passed the exam—that's a miracle!" or "It was a miraculous come-from-behind victory!" or *Miracle on 34th Street.* None of these comes close to the truth of what a miracle actually is.

A miracle is a supernatural event, an intervention in the natural universe by God. A miracle is a mighty work that you cannot do on your own, that could only be done by the power of God.

A lot of people who don't necessarily believe in Jesus still believe in miracles and the supernatural. The success of the television shows *Touched by an Angel* and *Joan of Arcadia* are proof of that.

Some of the most treasured works from literature and movies also key in on supernatural events. Two holiday classics come to mind: Ebenezer Scrooge's Christmas Eve transformation in *A Christmas Carol* and George Bailey's glimpse of the world if he had never been born in *It's a Wonderful Life.* Part of what makes these stories so poignant is our knowledge that things like that don't happen in "real life." In real life, we suppose, Scrooge would have bullied along to his tragic end, despised

Christ was a miracle. Every Christian is a miracle. Every answer to prayer is a miracle. Every divine illumination is a miracle. The power of Christianity in the world is a miraculous power. God help us to realize that ours is a High and Holy Calling.

—JOHN G. LAKE
(1870-1935)[1]

and alone. In real life, we critically consider, George Bailey would have drowned himself at wit's end.

I want you to see in these pages that miracles are *not* uncommon, they do happen in *real life*, and lives are amazingly transformed forever for the better, every day of the week. Miracles are an everyday occurrence for the people who walk in God's light.

From Genesis to Revelation, the Holy Bible is saturated with miracles. Many of these events not only changed the life of one man or woman but altered whole families and changed the course of history. When we say we stand on the Word of God, we declare we are standing on a history and tradition of astounding miracles, a record of God's supernatural power to intervene, rescue, provide, save, heal, and deliver. With this as our foundation, how could we ever doubt that miracles are a common event? God blesses and provides for His children through miracles. Further, God uses miracles to execute judgment upon His enemies and to bring about His plan and purposes in the earth.

As evidence of how very common miracles are, let's explore just a few of these life-changing, history-making acts of God from the Bible. This is not a comprehensive list, but it will give you an idea of just how common miracles are in the mind of God and the lives of His children. Now, if you are planning to follow God's call to begin operating in the miraculous, I urge you to read the Scriptures and see God's hand at work in each of the references here. It will amaze you and build your faith to see just what kind of everyday occurrence a miracle is for God and His children.

MIRACLES PERFORMED BY THE TRINITY

Creation. In Genesis 1 and 2, the first recorded miracle is that God— the Father, Son, and Holy Spirit—created the heavens and the earth, then went on to fill the earth with life and finish with His highest creation, man.

I heard a little story about a group of scientists who felt superior to God and thought they no longer needed His assistance. One of the scientists challenged God to a contest. He said, "Creation isn't such a big deal, God. I can make a man right now, the same way You did."

"Go for it," said God. The scientist began scooping up the clay to form his creation, and God quickly stepped in and said, "Wait just a minute! Go make your own dirt!" What the Trinity accomplished at Creation was to make something of nothing, a process that science has never duplicated.

The Flood. In Genesis 6:1—8:22 a series of miracles takes place: Animals come climb aboard Noah's ark; a worldwide flood wipes out the entire population of the earth when it had never rained before; then Noah, his family, and our entire species survive such a catastrophe. The rainbow we enjoy after a rain today is a miracle promise from God that such a punishment would never befall our earth again. Are you getting the idea that when the Triune God works a miracle, He pulls out all the stops?

The virgin birth of Jesus. Luke 1:26-38; 2:1-7 tells of the greatest miracle yet, for it brought into being the only perfect sacrifice for our transgressions, the Lamb of God who takes away the sins of the world. Only a Man without original sin, without *any* sin, could bridge the gap between man and God, so God had to send His own Son to be born as a man, but without the inherited sin of Adam. The King James Version says the Holy Spirit "overshadowed" Mary, appointing to her the task of delivering the Savior to the world.

The Transfiguration. Matthew 17:1-13 shows Peter, James, and John overwhelmed by this miraculous event. One minute they were praying with their leader, a rough Galilean carpenter, the next moment they saw Him revealed as He truly was, the Son of God, bathed in glorious light and conferring with two of His trusted human counselors, Moses and Elijah—both dead for centuries! Moses, as representative of the law, and Elijah, as representative of the prophets, discussed with Jesus "His decease which He was about to accomplish at Jerusalem" (Luke 9:31). No doubt their company gave comfort and grace to Christ as He faced His most terrible test, and it also gave His disciples a glimpse into His supernatural life beyond this life, to build their courage for the events that would soon transpire.

The Day of Pentecost. Before Jesus ascended into heaven, He promised His disciples He would send the Holy Spirit to abide with them forever. He didn't disappoint them. On the Day of Pentecost, suddenly, with a sound like a mighty rushing wind, the Holy Spirit came upon them, appearing like cloven tongues of fire. They all were filled with the Holy Spirit and received power to be His witnesses, to proclaim the Word boldly, and to launch the church triumphant. The book of Acts is a fascinating account of the many signs, wonders, and miracles performed by the early church as a result of the indwelling power and presence of the Holy Spirit.

MIRACLES PERFORMED BY INDIVIDUALS
IN THE OLD TESTAMENT

Deliverance of Israel from Egypt. The entire book of Exodus chronicles miracles performed by Moses and Aaron in their efforts to free Israel from Egypt and lead the Hebrew children to the Promised Land. Through God's miraculous power, Aaron's rod became a serpent, and Moses turned the water to blood and called down various plagues. At one point Moses spoke to a rock to make it pour out water for the people, and later he got mad and hit the rock with his staff, getting the same result, water from the rock. Perhaps the most dramatic miracle was Moses's parting of the Red Sea so the Israelites could walk across on dry land, then closing it to drown the pursuing Egyptians.

Joshua and the battle of Jericho. Joshua 6 tells the story of how the Israelite armies stormed the impenetrable walls of Jericho, not with their military might, but by following the orders God gave Joshua to march around the city once a day for seven days, and on the final day seven times, then shout their praises to God. And the walls came a-tumbling down.

Elijah prophesies and performs miracles. The two chapters of 1 Kings 17—18 showcase some miracles of the prophet Elijah. He prophesied a drought, and the rain immediately ceased. He prophesied a steady food source for himself and the widow of Zarephath, and they ate well while the rest of the countryside was starving. He raised the widow's son from the dead and, when the time was right, went to Mount Carmel for a face-off with the priests of Baal. He prayed down God's fire from heaven to consume his sacrifice while the Baal worshipers impotently stood by. Finally, he prayed for the rain to come again, and it did.

Elisha opens some eyes and blinds others. In 2 Kings 6, Elisha and his servant were surrounded on all sides by the vicious Syrian army, but Elisha was not at all perturbed and said, "Do not fear, for those who are with us are more than those who are with them" (2 Kings 6:16), and he prayed that God would open his servant's eyes to see the heavenly forces all around them: "The mountain was full of horses and chariots of fire all around Elisha" (6:17). Then Elisha prayed for the Lord to blind the enemy army and led the sightless soldiers himself to the king of Israel in Samaria.

The floating ax head. How about this uncommon miracle in 2 Kings 6:4-7? One of Elisha's servants borrowed an ax, and while he was working it slipped off the handle and sank into the Jordan River. What to do?! Elisha merely threw a stick in the water and commanded the ax head float to the top. He then told the servant to just reach out and pick it up. Simple.

MIRACLES PERFORMED BY JESUS

Turning water into wine. John 2:1-11 records Jesus's first miracle at a wedding reception, where His mother instructed him to help the host who had run out of wine. Isn't it interesting to know that our Savior began His miracle-working career at a wedding party? This incredible miracle saved the host from embarrassment, and it shows me there is no need too small for Him.

Healing Peter's mother-in-law. In Mark 1:29-31, Jesus went home with Peter for dinner where Peter's mother-in-law was in bed with a fever. Jesus healed her, and she reacted just as we should when Christ touches us. She got up and served Him.

Healing a leper. Mark 1:40-42 tells how a leper came to Jesus for help. Jesus had begun His public ministry and was preaching in synagogues throughout Galilee. The leper heard of His powerful ministry and believed that Christ could heal him. Moved with compassion, Jesus did!

Raising a dead man. John 11:1-44 says that Jesus was easily within a day's walk of Bethany where Lazarus lay dying when He received the news, yet He waited four days before going to visit. Lazarus was already dead and buried! But to show God's glory, Christ revived him.

Walking on water. Matthew 14:25 tells of another amazing miracle. Jesus knew His disciples would soon be traumatized by His arrest and crucifixion. To show them that He was Lord of all nature and to build their faith, He came to them in a storm at sea, walking on the water.

Restoring a severed ear. The miracle of Luke 22:50-51 occurred just after Jesus had spent that agonizing night in the Garden of Gethsemane. So desolate and overwhelmed was He, the Bible says His sweat came like drops of blood. When the soldiers arrived to arrest Him and begin the ordeal, one of Jesus's defenders drew a sword and struck off the ear of a man named Malchus. In the midst of His own suffering, Jesus had compassion and miraculously reattached it.

The apostle John said that Jesus did so many things that if every one of them should be written, the world itself could not contain all the books written about them (John 21:25). This list mentions just a few of the Lord's miracles and serves to show that for Jesus, operating in the miraculous was an everyday event. Further, after Christ's miracle-working ministry, miraculous resurrection, and the Day of Pentecost, the believers became miracle workers themselves, with supernatural events quite common among the members of the early church.

MIRACLES PERFORMED BY INDIVIDUALS
IN THE NEW TESTAMENT

Peter raises a woman from the dead. Acts 9:36-41 tells the story of Dorcas, or Tabitha, a beloved saint who had done much good for her church members in Joppa. Her death was a terrible blow to them, so they sent for Peter who called her back from the dead.

Paul's handkerchiefs heal. Acts 19:11-12 shows how God allowed Paul to work so many miracles that people began bringing him handkerchiefs to touch. When they placed the handkerchiefs on the sick folks "the diseases left them" (verse 12).

Paul raises a dead man. In Acts 20:7-12, an earnest young believer was sitting on the window ledge of a crowded upper room, listening to Paul preach until late in the evening. He dozed off, falling out the third floor window to his death. Paul went down and prayed over him and brought him back to life.

Miracles at Malta. Acts 28 records that on the island of Malta, Paul was bitten by a deadly snake with no ill effects. He prayed for the healing of a man suffering fever and dysentery, and when he was healed "the rest of those on the island who had diseases also came and were healed" (verse 9).

MIRACLES PERFORMED BY ANGELS

Angel of death. Isaiah 37:36 records how "the angel of the LORD went out, and killed in the camp of the Assyrians one hundred and eighty-five thousand; and when people arose early in the morning, there were the corpses—all dead" when their king Sennacherib came against the chosen people.

Preserving Daniel in the lions' den. Daniel 6:1-23 tells the story of Daniel who, when cast into a den of hungry lions for keeping his faith, was protected through the night when an angel shut the lions' mouths. What a night that must have been!

Troubling the waters. John 5:4 says that the pool of Bethesda was regularly visited by an angel who troubled the waters. The first sick person to plunge in while the angel was there received healing.

Rolling away the stone. Matthew 28:2 shows that although the authorities had secured the tomb of Jesus with a massive stone so that no one could steal the body and make false claims of a resurrection, that stone was no match for miracle-working angels.

Peter's deliverance from prison. In Acts 12:6-11, Peter was either still dreaming or in awe of the angel who came to set him free. The heavenly being struck the disciple to get his attention and jerked him up while telling him to get his shoes on and high-tail it out of there.

Herod's death. In Acts 12:23 an angel struck Herod dead. Herod was an all-around bad dude, but he went too far when he allowed the audience at his speech to proclaim his words those of a god and not a man.

Are you convinced by now that miracles are no uncommon thing for our uncommon God? They were performed by almost every good guy in the Bible: the Trinity, the Old Testament saints, Jesus, the New Testament saints, and angels. Let's look at just one of these "everyday" miracles from the first-century church. It is a compelling story that contains the basic elements you need to know to understand miracles, and we will refer to its components and the lessons we learn from it throughout this book. It concerns the healing of a lame man who was begging beside the temple gate called Beautiful:

> Now Peter and John went up together to the temple at the hour of prayer, the ninth hour. And a certain man lame from his mother's womb was carried, whom they laid daily at the gate of the temple which is called Beautiful, to ask alms from those who entered the temple; who, seeing Peter and John about to go into the temple, asked for alms. And fixing his eyes on him, with John, Peter said, "Look at us." So he gave them his attention, expecting to receive something from them. Then Peter said, "Silver and gold I do not have, but what I do have I give you: In the name of Jesus Christ of Nazareth, rise up and walk." And he took him by the right hand and lifted him up, and immediately his feet and ankle bones received strength. So he, leaping up, stood and walked and entered the temple with them—walking, leaping, and praising God. And all the people saw him walking and praising God. Then they knew that it was he who sat begging alms at the Beautiful Gate of the temple; and they were filled with wonder and amazement at what had happened to him.
>
> Now as the lame man who was healed held on to Peter and John, all the people ran together to them in the porch which is called Solomon's, greatly amazed. So when Peter saw it, he

responded to the people: "Men of Israel, why do you marvel at this? Or why look so intently at us, as though by our own power or godliness we had made this man walk? The God of Abraham, Isaac, and Jacob, the God of our fathers, glorified His Servant Jesus, whom you delivered up and denied in the presence of Pilate, when he was determined to let Him go. But you denied the Holy One and the Just, and asked for a murderer to be granted to you, and killed the Prince of life, whom God raised from the dead, of which we are witnesses. And His name, through faith in His name, has made this man strong, whom you see and know. Yes, the faith which comes through Him has given him this perfect soundness in the presence of you all." (Acts 3:1-16)

What a story! Peter and John were going about their business as they did every day. There was nothing special about that day, and yet suddenly they were given an opportunity to begin operating in the miraculous.

It would have been quite easy for the apostles to miss their appointment with destiny here. They had probably seen this man begging at the temple gate many times before; perhaps they had paid little attention to him on previous occasions. Their first response could have been simply to walk on by. That is probably what most people did.

Or perhaps, they could have decided to do the Christian thing, the charitable thing, and toss him a coin. They said they had no silver and gold, but in the previous chapter we read of the believers in Jerusalem after Pentecost: "Then fear came upon every soul, and many wonders and signs were done through the apostles. Now all who believed were together, and had all things in common, and sold their possessions and goods, and divided them among all, as anyone had need" (Acts 2:43-45).

The new church was sharing all its resources, from family to family, and there was a great respect for the apostles and the wonders they had performed. Do you think Peter and John couldn't have conjured up a few coins from the disciples to give this man? Or is it more likely that they weren't content with tossing him money when they knew that God had the power and will to completely heal him?

When Peter said, "Silver and gold I do not have," his real message was: money won't solve your real problem; what you need is a touch from God. The message is still true today. You can have a wad of hundred dollar bills in your back pocket, but the best gift you can give to a lame man is a touch from God. A few coins tossed his way would have made him grateful and fed him for a day, but proclaiming the Gospel to him and healing his affliction would change him for life.

Peter and John had been pursuing their normal daily activities, but they sensed when God wanted to interrupt their routine and do something *extraordinary* through the ordinary. This time, God wanted to publicly glorify His Son, Jesus, through an awesome miracle and then use the event to set the stage for Peter to preach the Gospel to all who were in the temple. And look at the result: "Many of those who heard the word believed; and the number of the men came to be about five thousand" (Acts 4:4).

We can easily imagine God's using Peter and John in such an extraordinary way because they were apostles, and after all, they had been with Jesus. But what about you and me? The Scriptures make it clear that it is still God's will and His good pleasure to work miracles through every single believer today. Remember, in the Great Commission Jesus clearly said that signs would follow *all those who believe*, not just apostles, pastors, or those who stand behind a pulpit (Mark 16:15-18). That means me, and it means you, if you believe.

If you are praying for a miracle right now, I believe this book will give you the plan to call it into reality. Now that you know what miracles are, we will take a look at *why* God allows miracles to happen, and you can discover whether the miracle for which you are praying is in line with God's six missions for miracles.

GOD'S SIX MISSIONS
for MIRACLES

EVERY MIRACLE HAS A MISSION. Yes, God loves you and wants you to be happy, but miracles often a have a purpose that is far beyond just providing you with immediate relief and comfort. There are many different missions for miracles that we discover in Scripture, and we'll discuss them over the next several chapters.

When you say that someone is on a mission, what you mean is that there is a purpose to what he or she is doing. We all know that NASA sent equipment to Mars to explore, take pictures, and find out whether or not there were any signs of life on the Red Planet. They spent millions on this expedition. There's no way they would have invested that kind of money had there not been a purpose behind what they were doing. They were on a mission.

The same is true with God. Everything He does has a purpose. Every miracle He performs has a mission. The validity of Christianity is based upon the miracle of the Resurrection. Just think about it. Everything we do and everything we believe as Christians is based upon the fact that our God is not in the tomb. Our God rose from the dead!

Just before He ascended to heaven, Jesus told His disciples to go to

A woman felt a special burden to pray for Reinhard [Bonnke]. As she began to intercede, she became aware that his life was somehow in danger.
She cried out to God, pleading, agonizing, wrestling in prayer until the burden lifted. Thousands of miles away in Africa the fever had broken and the crisis was over. It was at the same day and time that she had prayed for him.
—COLIN WHITTAKER[1]

Jerusalem and wait for the promise of the Father. They didn't know exactly what they were waiting for, but they gathered in the upper room in obedience to the Lord's command to wait.

Little did they know that God was about to perform the first major miracle, since the Resurrection, of the first-century church! It was a miracle that would change their lives, the church, and the world forever: Pentecost. This miracle produced a swirl of activity and added three thousand people to the church in one day. There was nothing coincidental about it and no doubt that it was a well-calculated event with a clear purpose. This miracle was on a mission!

He came with the sound of a rushing, mighty wind, tongues of fire that sat upon each believer, and an explosive power to praise God in languages unknown! The glorious evidence of God's presence spilled over from the upper room to the streets below. Look at the reaction:

> And when this sound occurred, the multitude came together, and were confused, because everyone heard them speak in his own language. Then they were all amazed and marveled, saying to one another, "Look, are not all these who speak Galileans? And how is it that we hear, each in our own language in which we were born? Parthians and Medes and Elamites, those dwelling in Mesopotamia,

Judea and Cappadocia, Pontus and Asia, Phrygia and Pamphylia, Egypt and the parts of Libya adjoining Cyrene, visitors from Rome, both Jews and proselytes, Cretans and Arabs— we hear them speaking in our own tongues the wonderful works of God." So they were all amazed and perplexed, saying to one another, "Whatever could this mean?" (Acts 2:6-12)

"Whatever could this mean?" I love that question, because it shows so clearly that everyone in hearing range knew that something incredible had occurred. No one had to convince them. Their curiosity was aroused, they had questions, and they weren't afraid to ask. They understood that this incredible happening wasn't happenstance but must have a greater meaning beyond what they could comprehend at the moment. By asking, "Whatever could this mean?" they were seeking to identify the mission, the purpose behind this miraculous event.

Right now, you and I are going to ask the same question and discover the purpose behind everything God does in the miraculous.

MISSION #1

Protect His People

AS WE BEGIN OUR STUDY of God's missions for miracles—the purpose behind everything God does in the miraculous—we'll start with the first mission: protection.

OLD TESTAMENT MIRACLES OF PROTECTION

God began His brilliant history of miracles of protection way back in the very beginning of man. In Genesis 4:15, we read of God placing a mark on Adam's son Cain to protect him from anyone claiming vengeance against him. Then in Genesis 6–8, God preserves the human race by miraculously saving Noah and his family from the great flood. In Genesis God also protected his friend Abraham as he traveled far from his homeland seeking the promise of an everlasting kingdom, and, by the miraculous acts of two angels, protected Abraham's nephew Lot from the destruction of Sodom and Gomorrah. God even sent an angel to protect Sarah's maid Hagar and Abraham's illegitimate son, Ishmael (Genesis 16).

Perhaps you know the story: Abraham and Sarah were impatient waiting for God's timing to fulfill His promise of a son for them, so they conspired to speed things along by having Abraham make a baby with

Sarah's maid. Although this was a sin in God's eyes, He still miraculously protected the maid Hagar and her unborn child, Ishmael. God will use His miraculous powers even to protect us from our own mistakes! Abraham made a lot of mistakes, including the one in Genesis 20 where he failed to tell a foreign king who fancied Sarah that Sarah was his wife! The king took her into his harem, but thankfully God miraculously intervened to save her.

The most dramatic miracles of protection in the Old Testament must be found in Israel's deliverance from Egypt. First there were the plagues, designed to force the Egyptians to accede to Moses's pleas for his people's freedom. These culminated in that dreadful night that the firstborn of every family in the nation was stricken with death—except for the Israelite slaves who had followed the Lord's instructions to paint the blood of their sacrificial Passover lamb upon their door posts. By this sign, the Lord knew to pass them by and protect their firstborn from death.

Finally, Pharaoh agreed to release the people of Israel, but then the Bible says he changed his mind and brought his armies chasing after them as they cowered on the banks of the Red Sea. The people were terrified. They would either be driven into the depths of the sea, or they would be slaughtered or captured by the armies. But Moses boldly told them, "Do not be afraid. Stand still, and see the salvation of the LORD, which He will accomplish for you today. For the Egyptians whom you see today, you shall see again no more forever. The LORD will fight for you, and you shall hold your peace" (Exodus 14:13-14).

Sure enough, the Red Sea parted like a Cecil B. DeMille movie extravaganza, and the people of Israel walked to freedom on dry land! When the angry Egyptians tried to follow, the sea rushed in on them and drowned them all. This is a powerful example of how God used a miracle to protect His people. And there are many more such examples throughout the Old and New Testaments. Let's look at one miracle of protection from the first-century church.

NEW TESTAMENT MIRACLES OF PROTECTION

In Acts 12:1-11, we find the story of Peter's miraculous protection. Herod had just had the apostle James beheaded, and he saw that it brought great pleasure to the religious authorities of the day. They had hoped that Jesus's death would stop His teachings from spreading and shatter the solidarity of His disciples. Instead, the disciples began boldly preaching the resurrection of the Savior. Far more people were turning to Jesus since He had ascended to the Father than had followed Him when He walked the earth. Many of the priests and Pharisees were disgusted by this, and when they could get the Roman government to execute apostles, they were all for it.

So Herod set his sights on Peter and had him arrested with the intent of having him killed. The night before his trial, Peter was fast asleep in his prison cell, bound and chained between two guards, no less! In the middle of the night, an angel appeared, loosed Peter from his chains, and conducted him safely out of the prison, past two check-points and through the iron gate of the city. The whole time his miracle was happening, Peter thought he was having a vision. When he came to himself, he realized that God had sent an angel to rescue him from certain death at the hand of Herod.

What a tremendous deliverance by the hand of God! It reminds me of His promise of protection in Psalms:

Because he has set his love upon Me, therefore I will deliver him;
I will set him on high, because he has known My name.
He shall call upon Me, and I will answer him;
I will be with him in trouble;
I will deliver him and honor him.
With long life I will satisfy him,
And show him My salvation. (Psalm 91:14-16)

You can probably recount at least one instance where God miracu-lously delivered you or someone you know from impending danger: a potential accident, a natural disaster, or other situation where you were in harm's way. And God only knows how many times He has delivered you from danger, or even death, that you didn't even know about.

Have you heard the stories of the 9/11 survivors, people who were supposed to be in the Twin Towers but for whatever reason didn't make it in that day? I read that one fellow was stuck in traffic because of a car accident and was late to work; another had to stop and buy a Band-Aid because his new shoes had made a blister, so he didn't get to work at the time he had hoped to. These seem like little things, but they could have been miracles of protection, too. Only God knows.

Have you ever seen the classic print of children playing on a bridge with their guardian angel hovering close by? Perhaps the angel had just prevented one of them from stumbling into the dangerous water below. In the painting, the children were unaware of God's protecting power. Yes, when we get to heaven, I am sure we will be amazed to realize the number of times God performed miracles on our behalf to protect us from harm.

Every miracle has a purpose, and some of those miracles have the specific purpose of protecting God's people. You may even have been on the receiving end of such a miracle, and you don't even realize it. But one thing I can guarantee you: When you do witness a miracle, there is another purpose it fulfills. It builds your faith. We'll discuss that next.

3

Mission #2

Produce Faith

Do you ever watch figure skating during the Olympics? It's an exciting event to watch, and I often marvel at the incredible grace as well as the strength and raw athleticism exhibited in the leaps, lifts, and other acrobatics on the ice. But you can hardly watch the events without holding your breath for fear that the athletes might overbalance just the tiniest bit and go spinning across the ice on their faces or backsides. For me it's just painful to watch.

Do you know there's a way to keep your heart from racing during those programs, a way you can be perfectly confident that your favorite skater isn't going to dash your hopes for her and humiliate herself? It's by watching her practice. If you get the chance to see her make those same moves, over and over, perfect every time, then you start to believe that yes, she can also do that in competition.

Some of those leaps and landings look like impossible feats when you see them for the first time, but when you see your skater perform them for the hundredth time, it looks pretty easy, really.

When you see the impossible done once, it's a lot easier to believe in the impossible happening again. God knows that once you witness

This woman who…had been blind for four years…could see again. When the congregation realized what had happened, they erupted into a bedlam of excited shouts of praise and rejoicing….

In that atmosphere it seemed that anything could happen, and it did.

—Colin Whittaker[1]

your first miracle, it is easier for you to believe for your second miracle. And that brings us to the second mission of a miracle: produce faith.

God will sometimes use a miracle to produce faith in your life so that He can manifest His power through you. No matter how long you've known the Lord or how God has used you in the miraculous, you could always use more faith. Jesus did a rather funny miracle to illustrate this and produce faith in the lives of His apostles. You can find it in Mark 11.

And seeing from afar a fig tree having leaves, He went to see if perhaps He would find something on it. When He came to it, He found nothing but leaves, for it was not the season for figs. In response Jesus said to it, "Let no one eat fruit from you ever again." And His disciples heard it…. Now in the morning, as they passed by, they saw the fig tree dried up from the roots. (Mark 11:13-14, 20)

Now, what gives, Jesus? That tree wasn't bothering the Savior. In fact, He was being silly to look for fruit on it when it wasn't fig season. So why did He curse it? Remember, there is a mission for every miracle God performs, so there must have been a reason for Jesus to curse the fig tree.

There's another famous passage of Scripture where Jesus talks about our ability, indeed our mission, to bear fruit for Him. In John 15, Jesus makes clear that we are called to bear fruit for the kingdom and that we can only bear fruit for Him when we are permanently abiding in Him and His

Word. For Jesus, fruit-bearing plants were a symbol of the lives of His beloved children, but when He came to this particular fig tree, He searched and searched for fruit but found only leaves. He wasn't looking for leaves—He was looking for fruit!

Many Christians are like that bushy fig tree, full of the outward appearance of Christianity. They sure look good, like a nice healthy specimen of a believer, but rattle those branches and there's no fruit. God Himself is the Fruit Inspector, and He is looking for the fruit of righteousness, character, integrity, compassion, and forgiveness. He is looking for the fruit of the Spirit in our lives. He is looking for the fruit that lasts (John 15:16) of lost people who have been brought into the kingdom. He is looking for the fruit of a life full of good works that glorify Him.

The fig tree represented a fruitless life, and Jesus cursed it so that it withered. But the story doesn't end there. Jesus used the miracle of the fig tree to produce faith in the disciples. When Peter pointed out the withered tree to Jesus and reminded Him of His curse, Jesus said:

> Have faith in God. For assuredly, I say to you, whoever says to this mountain, "Be removed and be cast into the sea," and does not doubt in his heart, but believes that those things he says will be done, he will have whatever he says. Therefore I say to you, whatever things you ask when you pray, believe that you receive them, and you will have them. (Mark 11:22-24)

Jesus taught by precept and example. In other words, He would teach on a principle then demonstrate it. Or He would perform a miracle and then use it to teach about the kingdom of God. He used the miracle of the fig tree to teach His disciples a powerful lesson about bearing fruit and to demonstrate that if they had faith in God, their faith could move mountains. They had seen a "little" miracle like the cursing of the fig tree, but Jesus used it to build their faith for a *big* miracle, like the moving of a mountain!

(Note that as Jesus taught His disciples about faith to move mountains, He didn't say it was their faith alone that brought about the action, but He instructed them to *articulate* their miracle, to say, "Be removed and be cast into the sea." He was showing them how to *speak* their miracle into existence, as we will later be discussing in chapter 11.)

I was involved in the revival in Argentina for many years and saw many miracles, signs, and wonders. These are the very things Jesus predicted for those who follow Him, so to the believers in Argentina, they were not surprising. However, it is interesting to note that American Christians are thrilled to hear about miracles in Argentina and other countries but are sometimes skeptical of them in the U.S.A. The Brownsville Revival, centered in Pensacola, Florida, went on for years, and on an almost daily basis, we witnessed miracles of healing, deliverance, salvation, and more. It blew everybody away! Even people who had been praying for revival for years were amazed by what happened.

Why did the Spirit of God shake that place with such force and such physical evidence of the existence of the spiritual realm? I believe one reason was to build our faith for the coming end-times revival. I believe it was setting the stage for true believers to say: This is the time for signs and wonders. This revival we've heard about *can* happen and *will* happen.

When Jesus's disciples asked Him about the sign of His coming and the end of the age, He gave them a laundry list of things that would happen before His return, the most potent of which was this: "And this gospel of the kingdom will be preached in all the world as a witness to all the nations, and then the end will come" (Matthew 24:14). The Gospel message *will* be preached in all the nations—our Savior has decreed it—but how can it happen?

We cannot cram all the people of the world into a stadium. We cannot reach every third-world nation on a TV broadcast. We cannot fit all 6 billion people on the front row of a healing crusade, no matter how big the stage and how powerful the speakers. We are going to do our best by God's grace, and we are going to fill the football arenas and baseball fields with crusades and music and preaching. But that isn't going to reach every creature as Jesus commanded. That's only going to reach the millions who can get to the stadium or who have a TV to watch the broadcasts. But to reach them all will take something more.

The only conceivable way for this Gospel to be preached in every nation is for ordinary believers like you and me to begin operating in the miraculous from day to day. Then our neighbors in our little sphere of influence will start flocking to us so they can hear our message. Laypeople and ministers alike need to start claiming God's promises and operating in the miraculous so that the lost of the world run to them.

Don't worry, Jesus our Savior once was human like we are. He understands that we don't have the faith to believe for something big until we at least see the evidence of something small. He uses one miracle to build our faith for the next miracle. This is happening now in my church, Heartland Fellowship, in the Dallas/Fort Worth metroplex.

When our congregation started doing the study that was the basis for this book, one little miracle would spark faith for a slightly bigger miracle, and that miracle would spark the faith for the next miracle. In the chapters to come, I am going to share some of those true miracle stories with you, and I believe *your* faith is going to be built up to the point that you are believing for your own miracles, too!

And nothing succeeds like success. Once you begin operating in the miraculous, you won't ever want to go back. And once God begins using you to operate in the miraculous, you will want to share His love and His power with all those around you, becoming part of that endtimes revival Jesus predicted! You will find the miracle has produced faith in you, and now you want to promote what God has done for you, which is the next purpose for miracles that we will discuss, in chapter 4.

4

MISSION #3

Promote His Plan

I GUESS I AM A NATURALLY CURIOUS GUY. I am always asking questions. My most frequent question is *why?* I use this one on my church all the time. Why do we have Sunday school? Why do we meet on Sunday mornings? Why do we have a sermon? Why do we sing together? Why, why, why? I like to get them thinking about what we are doing and the reasons behind it. In that light, I think it is very healthy to ask questions, and it turns out it's okay to ask God questions, too. The disciples were like me. They had questions.

Now as Jesus passed by, He saw a man who was blind from birth. And His disciples asked Him, saying, "Rabbi, who sinned, this man or his parents, that he was born blind?"

Jesus answered, "Neither this man nor his parents sinned, but that the works of God should be revealed in him. I must work the works of Him who sent Me while it is day; the night is coming when no one can work. As long as I am in the world, I am the light of the world."

When He had said these things, He spat on the ground and made clay with the saliva; and He anointed the eyes of the

Healing is marvelous, but the greatest miracle is the transformation of a soul from darkness to light. I do not care if I never see another body healed, as long as I know that there are souls being saved. Healing of the body is nothing compared to the healing of the soul.

—KATHRYN KUHLMAN (1907-1976)[1]

blind man with the clay. And He said to him, "Go, wash in the pool of Siloam" (which is translated, Sent). So he went and washed, and came back seeing. (John 9:1-7)

The saying is that there are no stupid questions, but here it seems the disciples asked the *wrong* question. If they had thought for three minutes about the question they were asking, they would have known the answer to at least half of it anyway: how could the man's sin be responsible for his blindness if he was, indeed, born blind? He could not have consciously sinned before he was even born. And Jesus doesn't endorse their idea that his parents could be at fault because of *their* sin. It seems sometimes bad things do happen to good people.

The disciples were asking, "Why is this man suffering?" when they should have been asking, "What is Your intent in healing this man?" Jesus answered both questions. But what I love is the way He refocused their attention from the man and his problem onto what God wanted to do in the midst of it. It was as if Jesus were saying, "Hey guys, lift up your vision. There's something bigger going on here than assigning blame about why this man is blind. There's a purpose for his blindness, sure: it is to manifest the works of God when he is healed! I'm going to heal this man, and his healing will testify of Me and bring glory to My Father."

This then is the third mission of a miracle: promote God's plan.

God will often perform a miracle to promote His plan for the furtherance of His kingdom here on earth.

Some of the miracles I have already mentioned show this intent. For instance, in the Old Testament, it was not God's plan to let humanity end in the Flood, but He did want a fresh start for His children, so He rescued Noah and his family. It was not God's plan for the children of Israel to remain in bondage to Egypt, so He miraculously delivered them to a heritage of freedom in Canaan. It was not God's plan for Queen Jezebel to lead Israel into complete bondage to false gods like Baal, so He miraculously empowered Elijah to call down fire from on high (1 Kings 18).

In the New Testament, we see even more clearly that every miracle God delivers to further His plans also involves the destiny of eternal souls. When Peter was delivered from prison, of course it was God's plan to protect him, but He was also setting on the mission field one of the most prolific early evangelists who would win thousands to Christ, and whose writings would continue to encourage believers like you and me, even today.

Or look at the militant anti-Christian Saul on the road to Damascus. It took a miracle to turn him around. In Acts 9, we read about Saul on his journey with official documentation authorizing him to track down and imprison Christians for their heretical beliefs, but the Bible says:

> As he journeyed he came near Damascus, and suddenly a light shone around him from heaven. Then he fell to the ground, and heard a voice saying to him, "Saul, Saul, why are you persecuting Me?"
>
> And he said, "Who are You, Lord?"
>
> Then the Lord said, "I am Jesus, whom you are persecuting. It is hard for you to kick against the goads."
>
> So he, trembling and astonished, said, "Lord, what do You want me to do?"
>
> Then the Lord said to him, "Arise and go into the city, and you will be told what you must do."
>
> And the men who journeyed with him stood speechless, hearing a voice but seeing no one. (Acts 9:3-7)

Over in another part of the city, God was preparing a disciple to come and pray over Saul. The man was justly afraid to go, because he knew about Saul's reputation for hating Christians and the license he had to arrest them, but in a vision God gave him the assurance that all would be well. And from this miraculous intervention in the life of Saul, another powerful evangelist, Paul the apostle, had his beginnings. The miracle was meant to save his soul and countless souls of others through his missionary journeys.

In Acts 28, Paul experienced another miracle. Shipwrecked on the island of Malta, he was helping to build a fire when a poisonous snake bit him. He should have died on the spot, but instead he shook the snake off into the fire and went on about his business. The people couldn't believe it. Nobody lived after being bitten by that particular snake. Due to this miracle of survival, Paul was elevated to a place where he was free to promote the Gospel throughout the island, although he was actually a prisoner of the Roman Empire at the time. God used this miracle to open the door for His message to reach the island of Malta.

Because I know that God's miracles always have a component of promoting His plan to save souls through Jesus, whenever I witness a miracle, I start asking, "Where is the cross in this? Where does the message of the Gospel come through here?"

I love the story of Philip the apostle. In Acts 8:5-8, we find that "Philip went down to a city in Samaria and proclaimed the Christ there. When the crowds heard Philip and saw the miraculous signs he did, they all paid close attention to what he said. With shrieks, evil spirits came out of many, and many paralytics and cripples were healed. So there was great joy in that city" (NIV).

It was going very well for Philip. People were responding to his preaching; he was doing signs and wonders, and a whole city was rejoicing because of the Good News he brought them. Then suddenly in verse 26, an angel told Philip, "Go south to the road—the desert road—that goes down from Jerusalem to Gaza" (NIV). I don't know about you, but I wouldn't particularly like leaving a city where I was involved in an awesome move of God to go and walk down something so desolate sounding as "the desert road."

But as I have told you, every miracle is about souls and not just throngs of souls like we saw coming to Christ in Pensacola or Argentina (or like Philip was seeing in Samaria). Sometimes the miracle is just for one soul, as in this case. Philip went down the desert road just in time to see an official of the Ethiopian government go by in a chariot. Philip raced to catch up with him and discovered that the man "just happened" to be reading a scroll, a prophecy from Isaiah about Jesus. It was the perfect opportunity for Philip to share the Good News with him, and he experienced the miracle of salvation and was baptized right there at the side of the road.

God is interested in performing miracles of healing, financial miracles, and divine deliverance, but He is *most* interested in bringing His children into a right relationship with Him.

Nonbelievers have brought their sick child on a gurney to me at a healing crusade and say, "This is my daughter, and she's dying. Please pray for her and heal her." I want nothing more than to see that girl raised up, but in my heart I know that the miracle *must* have its foundation in furthering the kingdom and bringing souls to Jesus. So sometimes I just turn to that non-Christian dad and say, "I am believing God to heal your daughter. But let me ask you something. What purpose would there be in healing her so she can live a long life if at the natural end of that life, she and her whole family are to be separated from Jesus and spend eternity in hell?"

What I want that father to understand is that God has a mission for miracles, and that mission always includes souls coming to Jesus and Christ being glorified. In almost every recorded miracle in the New Testament, the recipients are drawn closer to Christ. We never read about them going off to forget about Christ and live a sinful life. Rather, the miracle always brings the person closer to Jesus.

At Heartland Fellowship, when I was preaching the series on miracles that became this book, one of the women in our congregation got inspired. Jeanne, whose story I mentioned in the introduction of this book, knew from the Scriptures now that she could operate in the miraculous, and so she went to visit a friend in the hospital. Her friend was in a comatose state and everyone was preparing for the worst. The patient was on life support, and her physicians were advising that the family go ahead and suspend life support, because there was no hope that she would ever regain consciousness.

So Jeanne walked into the hospital room, saddened because she knew that very soon they were planning to pull the plug, and she started to feel a little embarrassed and afraid.

After all, she was not a minister, and she had never been part of a miracle. She was not Benny Hinn or any other famous evangelist; she was a computer programmer. But her pastor had told her God wanted to work miracles through her, so she said to the family, "Can we sing a song? I would like for us just to worship God." And she led them in singing, "I am the Lord that healeth thee..." Then she prayed, and all of a sudden, her friend's eyes popped open! She looked up and said, "What's going on?"

Amazed and thrilled over what had just happened, Jeanne said, "Jesus is here to touch you." And she led her friend to make a commitment to Christ, right there in the hospital!

God had a mission in mind for that miracle: He knew the patient's time was running out, and He wanted to see her come to Christ before she drew her final breath. In fact, within hours, she slipped back into a coma and died. When Jeanne told me this story, I remember comforting her with the fact that she had been used of God in performing the greatest miracle of all. The whole purpose of her miracle was simply to give her the opportunity to come into relationship with Jesus and find heaven in her future.

Then there *are* what we might term "negative" miracles. In Acts 5, we find a miracle that, on a scale of one to ten, rates at the bottom of most people's list of favorite miracles. It is the tragic story of Ananias and Sapphira. In the previous chapter, we read that the believers had all things in common and that many of them sold their land and possessions then gave the money to the apostles for distribution to all who were in need. In fact, Barnabas in particular is named in honor for selling his land and bringing the money for the provision of the church (Acts 4:36-37).

Maybe Barnabas gave a large amount; we don't know why he in particular was called out, but it seemed to have affected Ananias and

Sapphira. Perhaps they wanted the same kind of adulation that Barnabas received for his contribution, or perhaps they genuinely wanted to help. They sold a piece of their property, and Ananias brought *some* of the money to the apostles. That was his right—the apostles weren't requiring anyone to give anything—and if Ananias wanted to give one-third of his profits, or one-half, or three-quarters, that was up to him. The problem was that for some reason he told Peter he was giving the entire amount of the sale. He lied about how much he had made in the sale, apparently not wanting anyone to know he and Sapphira were keeping back something for themselves.

Peter, led by the Holy Spirit, said to him,

> Ananias, how did Satan get you to lie to the Holy Spirit and secretly keep back part of the price of the field? Before you sold it, it was all yours, and after you sold it, the money was yours to do with as you wished. So what got into you to pull a trick like this? You didn't lie to men but to God. (Acts 5:3-4, MSG)

Immediately after Peter made this pronouncement, Ananias fell dead. Later, the Bible says his wife, Sapphira, arrived, apparently unaware of her husband's death, and also lied about the amount of the land sale. And she, too, dropped dead. They weren't stricken for lying to the other believers, but Peter said they had lied to the Holy Spirit. It seems like a stiff price to pay for them, but we must look at the bigger picture and understand that God's judgments carry a divine purpose.

Look at what happened as a result: "So great fear came upon all the church and upon all who heard these things. And through the hands of the apostles many signs and wonders were done among the people. And they were all with one accord in Solomon's Porch" (Acts 5:11-12). Was it just a coincidence that God used the apostles to perform many signs and wonders right after what happened to Ananias and Sapphira? The answer is no. God was on a mission. He had a purpose.

God was getting ready to perform incredible signs and wonders through the apostles. But first, the people had to know that they could not touch the holy things of God with unclean hands. In essence, He was saying, "This body of believers is My baby, and it is precious to Me, so keep your unclean hands off this child." It was a radical indication that God was totally serious about our lives honoring Him in every way if we were going to bear the name of Christian in honor of His Son.

Now you know that miracles have a purpose, not only of protecting God's people and producing faith, but also of promoting God's plans. But my very favorite mission of a miracle to talk about is the one we'll examine in the next chapter, and it's probably one that you have never considered before!

5

MISSION #4

Propose to His Beloved Bride

A MAN WILL GO TO GREAT LENGTHS TO PROPOSE to his bride. Crazy with love, he wants to sweep her off her feet, to be her knight in shining armor. Here are just a few of the creative proposals I've heard of:

I heard of a fellow who rented a billboard on the way to his girlfriend's office: "Susie, I love you. Will you marry me?" Susie was blown away!

I've noticed the folks in Texas take their sports teams and school loyalty very seriously. One young man took his gal, an alumnus, to the Texas A&M football stadium, where on the fifty-yard line he had displayed an Aggie jersey with the words "Will you marry me?" across the shoulders. His fiancée was surprised and delighted.

Another fellow took his girl to dinner at a posh restaurant in New York City then conducted her to the helicopter he had hired so they could see the lights of the city at night. Hovering above the Statue of Liberty, he produced the ring from his pocket and popped the question.

A good friend who helped me with organizing and writing this book told me how her husband proposed—underwater. Since I am a certified diver, the story immediately captured my interest. They are both scuba diving instructors, and he told her on one dive that a mutual friend wanted to shoot underwater video of some divers exploring a shipwreck. When they arrived at the dive site, thirty-five feet underwater, he knelt on the sandy bottom of the sea and extended an underwater slate to her on which he had written, "I love you. Will you marry me?" (Their friend *was* shooting video of the dive, and it's hilarious. She read the slate and began to laugh, which caused her scuba mask to flood. While she was trying to clear her mask, her new fiancé was trying to jam an engagement ring onto her hand.)

My own proposal story isn't what you would call romantic. My wife, Jeri, and I were attending David Wilkerson's Bible school in Lindale, Texas. Dating wasn't allowed at the school—in fact, one of the rules was actually "no falling in love." However, we did fall in love, and we went to the school leadership to confess it. They realized this was part of God's plan, but to protect us they put us on restriction. We were only allowed to see each other for fifteen minutes a day, and we were not allowed any other contact. We couldn't touch each other, and we couldn't even write notes to each other.

We had never had a date. We had never held hands. We had never kissed. But I loved her so much, and I knew I wanted to marry her. When the moment arrived to ask her to marry me, we were, of course, still on restriction. We had our fifteen minutes to share that day, and I asked her to take a walk with me. The Bible school was situated on a big ranch, so there was no candle-lit dinner table, no roses—I couldn't even afford a ring! Instead, we walked out into a field, where the smell of manure was wafting toward us from the cattle barn.

About five minutes into our walk, we leaned up against a fence, and I said to Jeri, "Baby, I love you."

"I love you, too," she replied.

Then I said, "Will you marry me?"

She responded, "After all we've been through, how can I say no?"

"You will?" I asked.

"Yes," she replied.

So we got engaged, and I couldn't even shake her hand because of those stringent rules. Our time was about up, so we just looked at each other and said, "Well, gotta go."

It wasn't a romantic proposal, but it did the trick, and Jeri and I have been happily married for over twenty-five years, as much in love today as we were back then.

Every man remembers how he proposed to his girl, and every girl remembers how her husband asked for her hand. The proposal is the way we guys want to overwhelm her so she can't say no. Did you ever think that a *miracle* is one way God proposes to us, His bride? He wants to overwhelm us with His love for us, and there's no better way to do it than with a miracle.

He shows His love with signs.

—CARLOS ANNACONDIA[1]

The Bible calls the church the bride of Christ. That being the case, Jesus has to propose to His bride. Christ's original proposal to His beloved outshines all the marriage proposals I just mentioned to you and any that we as men could dream up.

Two thousand years ago, Jesus proposed in the most dramatic display of love the world has ever seen. He endured horrific torture, died on the cross, and rose from the grave, all for the one He loves. His sacrifice on the cross saved us from our sins so we could have eternal life with Him, something no one else could do, and only someone who loved us with an awesome love would even consider doing. His death, burial, and resurrection are the greatest of all miracles, the most spectacular of all proposals, and the ultimate demonstration of true love.

Ephesians 5:25-27 admonishes,

> Husbands, love your wives, just as Christ also loved the church and gave Himself for her, that He might sanctify and cleanse her with the washing of water by the word, that He might present her to Himself a glorious church, not having spot or wrinkle or any such thing, but that she should be holy and without blemish.

Christ made that sacrifice, His proposal of undying love for us, so that He could present us to Himself as a pure and radiant bride. There is none of our work in it—we couldn't be pure enough for Him if we tried—but His holiness, grace, mercy, compassion, and forgiveness are so great that He did the work of the cross to present us to Himself a glorious church.

But that is just one—one ultimate!—miracle that Christ did to propose His love to us. Even today, He continues to use miracles as a way of proposing to His beloved bride. It was the same when Jesus walked the earth. He knew that people were stubborn when it came to receiving His love. His words so often fell to the ground without bearing fruit because of unbelief. But then came the miracles. The miracles caused even the hardest of hearts to melt and turn to Him. Look at the ways Jesus made clear this mission of a miracle:

> But if I do, though you do not believe Me, believe the works, that you may know and believe that the Father is in Me, and I in Him…. Do you not believe that I am in the Father, and the Father in Me? The words that I speak to you I do not speak on My own authority; but the Father who dwells in Me does the works. Believe Me that I am in the Father and the Father in Me, or else believe Me *for the sake of the works themselves.* (John 10:38; 14:10-11, italics added)

Jesus was saying, "Okay, you don't believe in Me because of what I say, so I'll prove to you what I am saying is true because I want you to be My bride." Then He would perform a miracle, and many would believe because of the miracle.

In the last chapter we read about the conversion of Saul of Tarsus. What was that if not a proposal? Saul had been persecuting Christians and throwing them in prison, thinking he was doing God a favor. God got his attention in a dramatic way on the road to Damascus, and for three days afterward Saul was blind. All the while, Jesus was wooing him, saying, "Saul, I love you. Be Mine." When Saul came to Christ, his sight was restored, and shortly thereafter he received a new name. He became the apostle Paul.

Later, in Acts 16, Paul and Silas were thrown into prison in Philippi because they had cast a demon out of a woman. At midnight, they were in their prison cell singing praises to God. The other prisoners heard them and, most likely, so could the jailer, but the jailer remained unmoved. He couldn't have cared less. But Jesus loved the jailer and wanted to propose to him. So what did He do?

While Paul and Silas were still praising the Lord, God sent a violent earthquake that shook the foundations of the prison. All the prison doors were opened, and everybody's chains came loose. The jailer, convinced the prisoners had all escaped—and that he would be held responsible for the jail break—drew his sword to kill himself! A quick suicide seemed better to him than facing the tribunal that would punish him for allowing all the prisoners to get away.

But Paul shouted, "Don't harm yourself! We are all here!"

The jailer rushed into the prison cell, fell trembling at Paul's feet, and cried, "Sir, what must I do to be saved?" The whole time, Jesus was on His knees, proposing to the jailer, saying, "I love you! I shook your whole world so I could get your attention and ask you to commit your life to Me."

Of course, I remember very clearly the day Jesus proposed to me. At that time my life had dissolved into drug abuse and addiction. By the age of twenty-one, my body was broken because of it. I was lying in my room in my mother's house, and it felt like every nerve ending was on fire with pain. I was convulsing in agony. I felt like I was dying. I believe to this day that I *was* dying.

But I had a couple things going for me, even in that pitiful state. One was my mom. She had never stopped praying for me all through the years that I had been breaking her heart, drinking and abusing drugs, constantly getting into trouble at school. My wild lifestyle led me to hitchhike across America looking for more narcotics. Regardless of how bad I was, Mom prayed and believed that God could and would save and transform me. The other thing I had working for me, despite my sinful life and shameful bondage to drugs, was that Jesus loved me and was just waiting for me to realize it.

When I think back to that day, I can almost feel the rending pain, almost smell the sick stench of sweat, almost taste the awful bile that was rising in my throat. It is such an odd contrast to know that Jesus was in that room saying to Himself, "This is the day! In ten more minutes, I'm going to pop the question to Steve."

The pain and convulsions had started on a Saturday, and throughout the ordeal, I had actually been considering suicide. I had heard of drug fiends like me dying in the agony I was experiencing, and I didn't want to go that way. I thought, at least if I killed myself the pain would be over. Then on Tuesday morning, October 28, 1975, my mom invited over a young Lutheran minister. I had met him once before and didn't give him the time of day. At that time I didn't care to hear what he wanted to tell me.

But that day I was all ears. He didn't really say much, just, "Steve, I can't help you, but I know Someone who can. His name is Jesus, and He's here to deliver you. Pray with me."

I couldn't pray. I was in too much pain. But I could just barely say the name of Jesus, and so I started to say it, over and over again. And Jesus heard me—He knew I was accepting His proposal. I felt His presence fill the room. In just a matter of moments the convulsions stopped, and the pain ceased! Not only that, but I felt brand new. The desire for drugs, the confusion, and the emptiness that had plagued me for years all disappeared.

Jesus performed a miracle of deliverance for me, and it was His way to declare His love and ask me to be His.

Maybe you came to the Lord in some dramatic fashion; maybe God sent you your own personal earthquake to get your attention. Perhaps your financial position shattered and tumbled to the ground, and all the securities you had counted on crumbled before your very eyes. As a result, you turned to the Lord. Or maybe you were sick, and God healed you when a believer prayed for you, so you accepted His proposal. Or maybe, like me, you were addicted to drugs, and God set you free.

That's God's proposal of love, and they keep happening all the time, because "the Lord is not slack concerning His promise, as some count slackness, but is longsuffering toward us, not willing that any should perish but that all should come to repentance" (2 Peter 3:9). God is proposing to His bride every day, and the reason is this: He loves us and does not want us to face eternity without Him. How awesome is our God!

6

MISSION #5

Prepare His People for Judgment

HERE'S A WILD EXPERIENCE THAT HAPPENED TO ME BEFORE I WAS saved. I was about nineteen years old and totally hooked on drugs. You could not pump enough narcotics into my body to satisfy me. I especially loved hallucinogenics—those drugs that alter or create false perceptions of sight, sound, and other senses—like psilocybin mushrooms. I was always on the hunt for anything that would send me on an hallucinogenic trip.

Now here I was a drug addict, wigged out of my mind—crazy, but I wasn't stupid. A friend and I were hitchhiking through Flagstaff, Arizona, and got ourselves a ride to Northern Arizona University, where I went to the library and looked up maps of the Navajo reservations. My plan was to discover the traditional Indian grounds where peyote cactus grew. Peyote is a plant the Indians used, and some are still using, in their religious rituals that is supposed to expand the mind. I had used mescaline, the drug derived from this cactus, but had never actually found it in its natural form.

Synthetic hallucinogens like LSD were illegal and expensive, but I figured peyote was growing wild and free. So I found these maps from the 1800s, made copies, and with my friend went to catch a ride to the reservation. Two high school boys in a pickup truck pulled over to give us a ride. We told them, "Hey, if you give us a ride to the Navajo reservation, we'll turn you on to some peyote." Those boys got all excited. They thought I was mature and wise because I was nineteen and hitchhiking across America in search of mescaline.

Back then, and I don't know if this is still true today, kids from Arizona thought it was really cool to drive to the California coast and spend their weekends or summer breaks on the beach. Those two boys were on summer vacation between their junior and senior year in high school, and they were going to California. I didn't know it at the time, but "sex, drugs, and rock 'n' roll" were the only things on their list for that summer. They were heading to California for the ultimate party. And when they heard we could hook them up with free hallucinogens, they were *in*.

The boy in the passenger seat got out and let my friend sit in the cab of the truck, while I climbed into the back with him. Then we started flying down the highway. Those high school boys sped us down the interstate at seventy miles an hour—what a ride! I had positioned myself in the back of the truck up on a wheel well, so the other boy decided to jump up onto the opposite one facing me.

All of a sudden, that young man leaped up from his spot and lurched across the truck to sit beside me. I had no idea what he was doing, and I don't think he even knew—maybe he wanted to be able to hear what I was saying better. But as soon as he dropped down next to me, there was a powerful blast like the sound of a ten-gauge shotgun going off. Suddenly, where that boy had been sitting about three seconds before, a yard-long piece of steel rebar shot up through the wheel well from the street. It had been lying on the road, and it was kicked up by the tires with such force that it drove up *through* the wheel well and went flying into the air.

That was a three-foot piece of steel, at least a half inch across, moving with such speed and power that it sailed into the air about a hundred yards and was still spiraling up when the truck came to a tire-screeching halt. In total shock, my friend and the driver stumbled out of the cab. We were all watching the metal rod spin end over end in the air and then drop back down to the roadside. I looked over at that boy, and his face was white as a sheet.

It was clear that if he had still been sitting on that wheel well for another few seconds, the rebar would have shot right up into him and out the top of his head before it went flying into space. It was a complete miracle that he had chosen to get up and move at that moment.

I was one freaked-out hippie. I just sat in the back of that truck, staring in disbelief. But those high school boys jumped back in and got moving. They drove directly to a church, ran up to the door of the parsonage where the pastor lived, and started banging on the door.

My buddy didn't really know what was going on, but I followed along behind the kids as the pastor walked them into the church. Within a few moments, both boys flung themselves down at the altar and started shouting out for forgiveness, crying to Jesus. They got saved! It was amazing.

At the time, it was all just spooky to me. I didn't get it. But now, looking back, I can see. God saved those boys from whatever trouble they had been planning to get into with an absolute miracle. And that brings us to the fifth mission for a miracle: preparation for judgment.

God will perform a miracle to prepare His people for His judgment to come.

This kind of miracle is one of the common ones in the Old Testament. In Daniel 5, we have the famous story of the handwriting on the wall. The setting is in the Babylonian Empire when the Jews were in exile from Jerusalem. The arrogant and wicked King Belshazzar was on the throne, and during a drunken feast he did an unthinkable and abominable thing. He ordered his servants to bring the gold and silver chalices that had

Even in the midst of the severest judgments, the underlying purposes of God are still those of grace and mercy.

—DEREK PRINCE
(1915-2003)[1]

49

been crafted and used as implements of worship in the Lord's temple in Jerusalem. His father, Nebuchadnezzar, had seized the chalices in the capture of Jerusalem and had put them in his treasury in Babylon earlier when he was king.

Belshazzar, his wives, and his friends all drank from the chalices, and they praised the gods of gold, silver, bronze, iron, wood, and stone. Suddenly, in the midst of their debauchery, God caused a man's hand to appear in the room and begin writing on the wall of the palace where they were assembled. The king saw this, and it terrified him to the point that his knees started to knock together and his legs gave way.

When the supernatural hand disappeared, the message was left boldly printed on the wall, but whatever it said, it was in a language the king could not read. That frightened him most of all. He could not pass it off as a drunken illusion, because the evidence was there on the wall. But what did it mean?

Belshazzar called together all his sorcerers and astrologers, promising a large reward and a place of honor to the one who could translate the message. But no one could. Then the queen remembered that the Hebrew Daniel had "the Spirit of the Holy God" (Daniel 5:11). They summoned him, and he interpreted the writing, which foretold the disastrous fate for the king and the Babylonian empire. Here was Daniel's interpretation:

> And this is the inscription that was written: MENE, MENE, TEKEL, UPHARSIN. This is the interpretation of each word. MENE: God has numbered your kingdom, and finished it; TEKEL: You have been weighed in the balances, and found wanting; PERES: Your kingdom has been divided, and given to the Medes and Persians. (Daniel 5:25-28)

So God warned His people about the coming judgment upon the Babylonians through the prophet Daniel. That very night Belshazzar was slain, and the kingdom was given to the Medes and Persians just as Daniel had foretold. What a classic example of God performing a miracle to prepare the people for His judgment.

The story of Jonah is also a record of God's desire to warn the lost to turn from their wicked ways and avoid judgment:

Now the word of the LORD came to Jonah the son of Amittai, saying, "Arise, go to Nineveh, that great city, and cry out against it; for their wickedness has come up before Me." But Jonah arose to flee to Tarshish from the presence of the LORD. He went down to Joppa, and found a ship going to Tarshish; so he paid the fare, and went down into it, to go with them to Tarshish from the presence of the LORD. (Jonah 1:1-3)

God wasn't kidding that Nineveh was a wicked city, and Jonah knew it. The people weren't Jewish, and there was a good possibility Jews were persecuted in Nineveh, so Jonah wasn't just afraid that no one would listen to his message of repentance; he was afraid that they would kill him for preaching it. No wonder he fled!

But God loved the people of Nineveh and so wanted to save them from their wickedness that He sent a storm to trouble Jonah's boat. The sailors, suspecting that Jonah was the cause of their turmoil, threw him overboard. Then God sent a huge fish to swallow Jonah. After three days in the belly of this creature, Jonah was spit up on dry land only to start his journey to Nineveh all over again:

Now Nineveh was an exceedingly great city, a three-day journey in extent. And Jonah began to enter the city on the first day's walk. Then he cried out and said, "Yet forty days, and Nineveh shall be overthrown!" So the people of Nineveh believed God, proclaimed a fast, and put on sackcloth, from the greatest to the least of them. (Jonah 3:3-5)

Through His prophet, God gave Nineveh forty days to turn or burn, and thankfully, they chose to repent and come to God for forgiveness. Jonah's story is a miracle with a mission: to save the people of Nineveh from judgment.

I heard the story of a Christian mom who had a compliant little boy and a strong-willed little girl. The little girl, before she was two years old, determined that she was a big girl and didn't need a car seat. She was such a pill and threw such tantrums that it was easier for her parents just to put her in the car with a seatbelt than to try to wrestle her into the car seat.

A few months later, long after the car seat had been retired, Mom had the notion to get it back out and start strapping her daughter in again. The little girl started throwing a fit, and in exasperation Dad told his wife just to forget it and stop making the child scream and cry. Mom was resolute and she strapped her angry baby into the car seat before they left that morning.

That very day a car smashed into Mom's car. Mom, brother, and sister all survived with just a few bumps and bruises, but it was obvious that if the little one had not been strapped safely into her car seat, she would have been instantly killed by the force of the collision. The three were taken to the hospital, and after Dad had seen that they were all right, he went to take care of the details of the accident. The car had been totaled.

When he saw the wreckage, he broke out in a cold sweat. Had it been only that morning he had been telling his wife *not* to put their precious daughter into her car seat? In tears he returned to his wife and apologized, promising always to support her when it came to protecting their children. God had miraculously saved his little girl, and he immediately repented of his former stubbornness and carelessness.

Maybe God has done a miracle in your life to prepare you for judgment to come. Maybe you yourself were in a car accident yet you walked away. Perhaps you decided at the last minute to not take that flight—before it crashed. Think carefully. Haven't you experienced an amazing bit of "luck" that you couldn't explain? What was it?

I'll tell you: it's a miracle. And if you haven't acknowledged it as such, you need to do that right now. If you haven't given Jesus complete control of your life, you need to do that right now. Because that miracle could have been God's way of preparing you for judgment, and you may not get off so easy the next time.

If you have been playing a game with Jesus trying to see how long you can go on living in sin, living without Him, maybe attending church and paying lip service to Jesus but not walking with Him, that has to stop. If that is your situation right now, I am begging you to heed this warning. Maybe it is a miracle that you are reading this right now, and God is calling to you in preparation for judgment that you can still avoid if you change your ways starting this moment.

It's easy to come into relationship with Jesus. The Bible says we all have sinned and fallen short of the glory of God (Romans 3:23). That simply means none of us can ever be holy enough on our own to come into the presence of God. Yet all of us need to come to Him, in order to have eternal life. How can we ever be made fit for relationship with Him?

Through Jesus. On the cross He allowed Himself to be punished for our sins. When we accept that gift and ask Him to forgive us for our sins, He washes us clean and makes us acceptable to God. We become His children.

Maybe you have heard the Gospel story many times. That was my case. And remember, I had even witnessed with my own eyes the dramatic miracle of that boy being saved from sure death in the back of that truck. But that was *his* miracle, and somehow it didn't connect with me. I wish it had; it would have saved me from two more years of misery and drug addiction. Don't be as foolish as I was! Accept the truth now. "Behold, now is the accepted time; behold, now is the day of salvation" (2 Corinthians 6:2).

Perhaps you *have* accepted Christ as Savior and yet you are not living according to His plan and will. This was the sin of the Hebrew children who knew full well the miracle-working power of their God and had experienced His supernatural provision. Yet again and again they turned away from Him. This unwillingness to walk in God's ways caused the entire generation that escaped from Egypt to die in the wilderness without ever experiencing the Promised Land! Only Joshua and Caleb from the "old guard" were allowed to possess the land, because they had remained faithful to God.

Believers today have been given much more than the Israelites. The Hebrew children received manna from heaven, water from the rock, miraculous rescue from Pharaoh, clothes and shoes that never wore out. But *we* have been given the very Bread of Life, salvation provided by Jesus Himself! He saved us, cleansed us from our sins, adopted us into His family. He gave us His Word as our guide, His Holy Spirit as our Comforter, and everything we need pertaining to life and godliness. We have been given so much, and Jesus said, "To whom much is given, from him much will be required" (Luke 12:48).

But just like the children of Israel, we can still fall into the same sins of idolatry, unbelief, immorality, murmuring, complaining, and the like. We are told in 1 Corinthians 11:28 to keep ourselves on the examination table. When we examine ourselves and take out those things that are wrong in our lives, we avoid the consequences of those sins.

I thank God that miracles still occur today and help us prepare for judgment to come. And this is further proof of the final mission of a miracle, which we'll discuss in the next chapter—to show that God is always in control.

7

MISSION #6

Prove He Is in Control

DO YOU KNOW WHAT THE FOUNDERS OF GOOGLE are worth? Do you even know what Google is? It's an Internet search engine that millions of people use to find information and products online. Apparently it's a huge moneymaker, because the two founders are worth $4 billion each. That's billions now, not millions.

But they are kind of on the low end of the billionaires' club. Microsoft founder Bill Gates has a net worth of $48 billion. Investor Warren Buffet has a net worth of $41 billion. Michael Dell, of Dell computers, is also slacking, with just $14 billion. Four members of Sam Walton's family, the Wal-Mart folks, are worth $18 billion each.

Have you ever thought about what you would do with that kind of money? If you don't like what your cook made for dinner, you could call the Four Seasons in New York and have something flown in. If you don't like your kid's report card, you could send the little rug rat to a boarding school in Switzerland to have him privately tutored to speak French, German, Spanish and a half dozen other languages. Surely people with that kind of money must be totally in control of their every circumstance. Maybe they have a house on every continent or a luxury yacht in every ocean. Maybe they have all their clothes tailor made, or maybe they can deck their wives out with crown jewels. I don't know.

But here is what I do know: Every person, rich or poor, is going to die someday. And when that happens, the size of their bank account and number of their stock options won't mean a thing to them. The only thing that will matter on their personal horizon is, did they know Jesus? Did they ask Him to forgive their sins?

On this earth, $1 billion—or $48 billion—may give you the power to control your circumstances to a point. But in the life to come, $48 billion might as well be toilet paper for all the good it will do you if you don't know God. And for better or worse, sometimes He uses a miracle to get this point across: ultimately, God is the One in control.

In this era of advancement, with all the mind-boggling technology of man, it's no wonder the world is full of people who are lifted up because of their accomplishment or status in life. They think because of their intellect, their education, their hard work, or their ingenuity they have achieved success. But our idea of earthly success is nothing compared to the Sovereign One who is Lord of All.

In a miracle, God for one moment shows Himself, that we may remember it is He that is at work when no miracle is seen.

—F. W. ROBERTSON
(1816-1853)[1]

He is the All-knowing One who knows all about the past, present, and future. He knows our every thought and motive and the word on our tongue before we ever speak. He has the answer to every question and holds the key to every mystery.

He is the All-powerful One who formed the universe by the power of His word. He is the One who gives us strength and ability to accomplish all the marvels known to man. He is the Creator of all things who formed mankind from the dust of the earth. He is the One who gives us the creativity to design and invent and to fill our world with beauty.

He is the Eternal One who lives forever, who gives us breath and holds our very days in the palm of His hand.

56

He is also the Giver of every good and perfect gift, the One who loves to bless His children.

In Control As Lord of All

Everything we have, and all that we accomplish, is because of Him. Even the miracle of His blessing upon our lives has a mission and a purpose. It's all for His glory and the advancement of His kingdom, and His constant presence assures us that He is always in control.

Lord of Life and Death

One of my favorite miracles of Jesus is His raising Lazarus from the dead. I have been in Israel, retracing the steps of the Savior. When Jesus received word that Lazarus was ill, He was only about an hour's walk from Lazarus's home in Bethany. But Jesus waited two days to go to Bethany. He was waiting for Lazarus to die.

Why would He do that? He loved Lazarus. Did he want him to die? No, but He said, "This sickness is not unto death, but for the glory of God, that the Son of God may be glorified through it" (John 11:4). Lazarus *did* die before Jesus arrived. And yet that wasn't the end of the story:

> Now Martha, as soon as she heard that Jesus was coming, went and met Him, but Mary was sitting in the house. Now Martha said to Jesus, "Lord, if You had been here, my brother would not have died. But even now I know that whatever You ask of God, God will give You."
>
> Jesus said to her, "Your brother will rise again."
>
> Martha said to Him, "I know that he will rise again in the resurrection at the last day."
>
> Jesus said to her, "I am the resurrection and the life. He who believes in Me, though he may die, he shall live. And whoever lives and believes in Me shall never die. Do you believe this?" (John 11:20-26)

When Jesus told Martha He was the resurrection and the life, He was assuring her, "I am in control of this situation because I control life and death itself." Of course, Jesus then went to the tomb and called for

Lazarus to come forth, and He came out, alive again. If Jesus had healed Lazarus during his terrible sickness, it would have been a great miracle. But raising him from the dead had an even greater mission: to prove to the people, and to you and me, that God is Lord of life and death.

LORD OF NATURE

In Luke, we read of the miraculous stilling of the storm on the Sea of Galilee (8:22-25). Jesus had asked the disciples to take Him to the other side of the lake. Sleeping peacefully in the boat when the squall blew in from nowhere to threaten their ship, Jesus never awakened when the wind began to howl and the waves pounded the boat.

In fearful panic for their lives, the disciples awakened Jesus and accused Him of not caring that they were going to die! He quieted the waves and storm with a word—and then rebuked the disciples for their lack of faith. And they were afraid and said to each other, "Who can this be? For He commands even the winds and water, and they obey Him!" (Luke 8:25). This miracle of calming the sea proved to the disciples that Jesus is Lord of nature.

LORD OF OUR LIVES

Sometimes God orchestrates what we might consider to be unusual circumstances to get our attention or to turn us in a different direction. This happened to Balaam in Numbers 22. The king of Moab had sent princes to ask Balaam, a prophet, to come and curse the invaders about to swarm over Moab. But the invaders were the children of Israel, and God told Balaam not to go with the princes and curse His people. Balaam saddled up his donkey to go anyway.

Along the way, the Angel of the Lord, seen only by the donkey, stood in their path. The donkey ran off into the fields to avoid the angel, then later crushed Balaam's foot into a wall trying to squeeze by him, and finally, caught in a narrow place with the angel directly in front of her, she simply lay down under Balaam. Infuriated, Balaam struck the poor donkey three blows. Then God enabled the donkey to speak!

> So the donkey said to Balaam, "Am I not your donkey on which you have ridden, ever since I became yours, to this day? Was I ever disposed to do this to you?"

And he said, "No."

Then the LORD opened Balaam's eyes, and he saw the Angel of the LORD standing in the way with His drawn sword in His hand; and he bowed his head and fell flat on his face. And the Angel of the LORD said to him, "Why have you struck your donkey these three times? Behold, I have come out to stand against you, because your way is perverse before Me. The donkey saw Me and turned aside from Me these three times. If she had not turned aside from Me, surely I would also have killed you by now, and let her live." (Numbers 22:30-33)

Before Balaam saw the angel, he seemed matter-of-fact about hearing his donkey speaking, didn't he? Maybe he sensed that this was the kind of miracle God used to turn a life in a different direction. Then he saw the angel and knew for certain that he was dealing with the Lord of his life. God allowed him to go on to Moab but then called on him to curse the Moabites and bless the chosen people.

Can you think of a time when your life took an unexpected turn and you wondered what God was doing or allowing to happen to you? But maybe now, in retrospect, you can see that in fact God's hand was moving in those events to bring you to the place He wanted you to be. It might not be as dramatic as having a conversation with your donkey, or maybe it was even more dramatic than that.

Understanding that God is in control of our lives brings a great sense of peace and assurance to our hearts and minds when we're in the midst of situations we don't understand. The next time life throws you a curveball, look up. Who knows, God may be performing a miracle in your life to prove to you once again that He is Lord of all and in total control.

Now that you understand God's purpose for miracles, you are ready to begin the practical steps of how you, personally, can begin to operate in the miraculous. In the next section, you will discover six keys to receiving miracles!

SIX KEYS *to* OPERATING *in the* MIRACULOUS

IF YOU WANT TO BECOME PRESIDENT OF THE UNITED STATES, there are certain requirements you have to meet. You have to have been born in the United States, you have to be at least thirty-five years old, and you have to win the election. These are key things in becoming president. And they don't happen overnight.

If you want to retire as a millionaire, you have to retain from your earnings or generate through investments a million dollars. It takes planning.

If you want to marry that beautiful blonde who sings in the choir, you are going to have to meet certain requirements: prove to her that you're a gentleman, win over her parents, and propose to her. Better have a good strategy in place. Every goal worth achieving in life begins with preparation, with planning, with meeting the requirements to be eligible for fulfilling the dream.

Operating in the miraculous is no different. If you want the power of God to flow through you, then you must learn what His Word has to say about the subject. There are certain steps necessary to prepare for a miracle, and there are steps required to receive a miracle.

These key steps will be explained in the six chapters of this section. These are the same steps Jesus had to take in order to perform miracles, the same steps the apostles had to take—and the same steps you can take to prepare yourself to operate in the miraculous and to receive miracles.

The miracle realm is a man's natural realm.... Sin dethroned man from the miracle-working realm...but grace is restoring the spirit to its place of dominion. When man comes to realize this, he will live in the realm of the supernatural without effort.

—JOHN G. LAKE
(1870-1935)[1]

8

KEY #1

Authority

To operate in the miraculous, you must first have the authority to work in the supernatural.

When you look at the miracle beside the temple gate called Beautiful in Acts 3, you notice that Peter and John did not simply tell the lame man to be healed. Rather they said, "In the name of Jesus Christ of Nazareth rise up and walk" (Acts 3:6). In so doing, Peter modeled the first key for preparing the way for a miracle: he indicated that he had the authority to do miracles.

Think about this: if you are speeding in your car on your way to work, and some clown in a red Volvo thinks you're going too fast, are you under any obligation to pull over and let him write you a speeding ticket if he waves at you or follows you? Of course not. He's just some clown in a red Volvo; it's not as if he is a patrol officer with the weight of the law behind him. What gives the police officer the authority to give you a ticket? It is conferred on him with the job—by the law and by our society.

This kind of authority that we as humans give to another human is natural authority, which is different from spiritual authority, authority given by God to certain people. But Romans 13:1 shows that *all* authority originates with God: "Let every soul be subject to the governing authorities. For there is no authority except from God, and the authorities that exist are appointed by God."

The principle of both natural and spiritual authority is the same: someone who has the power delegates that power to someone else. To have spiritual authority, we must receive its appointment from God. Jesus had received all authority from His Father over every principality and power, as He said in Matthew 28:18: "All authority has been given to Me in heaven and on earth."

In this passage, the Greek word for power is *exousia*, which means authority. It is the ability or strength by which one is endued to exercise power. It also means mastery, jurisdiction, strength, or force. More simply, it is power with the right or permission to use it. God the Father gave Jesus all power in heaven and on earth. He has total jurisdiction and authority over everything. Jesus then delegated that authority to believers.

What does this have to do with you and me operating in the miraculous? Everything. Jesus delegated authority and jurisdiction over demons, sickness, and all the works of the enemy—not just to anybody. He delegated the authority to operate in His power to those who are in a right relationship with Him: His disciples. In Luke 9:1-2, Jesus conferred upon His disciples the power and authority to cast out devils and cure the sick. In Matthew 10:1, Jesus delegated to His disciples the power to cast out demons and heal all manner of sickness and disease. In Luke 10:19, Jesus gave His disciples the power to tread on serpents and scorpions "and over all the power of the enemy, and nothing shall by any means hurt you."

Jesus gave this authority to His disciples. A disciple is a follower, or one who adheres to the teaching of his master. So in order for you to receive the spiritual authority Christ wants to give you, you must first be His disciple.

Who are Christ's true disciples? According to John 8:31, those who walk in obedience to His Word: "If you abide in My word, you are My disciples indeed." These words make it clear that the authority Jesus conferred upon His disciples wasn't just for the Twelve to whom He was speaking in the verses from Luke and Matthew, but rather for all who walk in His Word. The apostle Paul seems proof enough of that. He never met Jesus prior to Christ's crucifixion, resurrection, and ascension, and yet when he came into relationship with Jesus, he operated in the miraculous in mighty ways.

The problem with many believers today is that they don't have a relationship with Jesus. They may know the pastor, the deacons, or sing in the choir. They may have had a religious experience with Jesus at one time, but none of that matters if they are not in right relationship with Him today. You see, even the demons know the rules of spiritual authority, and the evil forces can spot a faker as quickly as you and I can spot junk e-mail.

It happened in the early church. The believers had developed a reputation for casting out demons in the name of Jesus. It worked so well, nonbelievers tried to do the same. But look what happened:

> Also there were seven sons of Sceva, a Jewish chief priest, who did so. And the evil spirit answered and said, "Jesus I know, and Paul I know; but who are you?"
>
> Then the man in whom the evil spirit was leaped on them, overpowered them, and prevailed against them, so that they fled out of that house naked and wounded. (Acts 19:14-16)

This demon was no dummy. He knew that those people calling on Jesus's name did not really have the authority of Jesus. They were no better than that clown in the red Volvo trying to give you a traffic ticket. They had no authority over him.

You and I must understand that in order to operate in the miraculous, we must be in right relationship with Jesus Christ. Otherwise, the spiritual world has no obligation to do anything except hinder and humiliate us. During the years that I ministered in Argentina in a nation-shaking revival marked by continuous signs and wonders, we faced many cases of demonic oppression. At one crusade we had one whole tent set aside for casting out demons. I had a visiting American pastor with me and asked him to come with me into the tent and cast out some demons. "No, not me, not right now," he said. "I'm not right with God." He honestly recognized that there was something in his life that was out of line with God's plan, and the last thing he wanted to do was try to exercise God's authority in that condition. He was wise.

Our relationship with Jesus Christ must be solid before we can have His authority to operate in the miraculous. Before we go on, I invite you to examine your relationship with Him.

This book is all about miracles, but the *greatest* miracle of all is something available to every single person, simply for the asking: the transformation of your heart, the salvation of your soul. I've heard people say, "I've known the Lord all my life," but what they really mean is that they have known *about* Him. They have been to church. They have sung the choruses. Sometimes they have even been baptized or confirmed in their faith. They may be very good, religious people, but they have never confessed Christ as Savior and come into a relationship with Him. As Keith Green used to say, "Walking into McDonalds doesn't make you a hamburger. Walking into church doesn't make you a Christian."

Maybe you have wandered away from the Lord; maybe you are doing things that Jesus would never do. Or maybe you have never really come into a relationship with Jesus Christ. You've been sitting in church, tapping your foot to the upbeat music and positive words without ever really connecting with the message that the power of Jesus is real and that it can change your life. Here's the real deal: no matter what you have done in your life or how you have sinned, Jesus can transform you and forgive you.

The Bible says every person has sinned and fallen short of God's glory. Because of that, we are permanently separated from God. But we are made in His image; we are His masterpiece, infused with His very essence. He created us to be in perfect harmony with Him, and we will never be truly satisfied or complete until we are in a right relationship with Him. The apostle Paul said that because of sin in this world "the whole creation groans and labors with birth pangs together until now" (Romans 8:22). No one can bring you peace except the Prince of Peace, and nothing can get rid of sin except the shed blood of Jesus.

Jesus suffered and died on the cross to pay the penalty for your sin. All you have to do to have those sins washed away and become a brand-new child of God is to acknowledge that gift and take Christ as your Savior. He is here to forgive you. The Bible says that if you confess your sins, He is faithful and just to forgive you and to cleanse you from all unrighteousness (1 John 1:9). If you are away from the Lord, and doing things that Jesus would never do, and you need forgiveness, pray with me now:

Dear Jesus, thank You for Your presence. Thank You for Your love. Thank You for not leaving me alone. I ask You now to forgive me. I have sinned. I'm sorry. Wash me, Jesus. Cleanse me. I repent. Make me new. Come live in my heart. Be my Savior. Be my Lord and my very best Friend. I give my life to You. From this moment on, I am Yours and You are mine. Jesus, come live Your life in me. In Your precious name. Amen.

Committing your life to Jesus Christ is the most important decision you will ever make. If you've prayed this prayer, I encourage you to get involved in a Bible-believing church where you can grow in God. I also can't stress to you enough the importance of spending time with the Lord on a daily basis in prayer and reading the Word. As you diligently pursue developing your relationship with Jesus, you will find the fulfillment and the purpose in life that you were created for.

Living in relationship with Jesus, you have come under His authority, and as His disciple, you have also been given His authority to operate in the miraculous on this earth. But keep in mind: this isn't a seven-steps-to-miracles book with step one being "Pray the prayer." You aren't going to be magically endowed with power because you've prayed to receive Christ as Savior. If you sincerely desire to live for Him and begin to learn His Word and follow His ways, you have indeed taken the first step. But if you just rushed through the prayer like an incantation so you can get on to the miracle-working part of the story, then you're acting like the clown in the red Volvo—you've strapped on a sheriff's badge and are now hoping you can write tickets. It won't work. You can't just claim to be a disciple, you must be one. And if you are, then you are ready to take the second step.

9

KEY #2

Anticipation

DO YOU REMEMBER that ketchup commercial that played the haunting strains of a pop song that said, "Anticipation—it's making me wait," while the hapless ketchup lover waited for the condiment finally to drip out of the bottle? The implied message was, this ketchup may be slow, but it is worth waiting for!

But there was another implication to the commercial which was more subtle, that of *no doubt.* Never once did that ketchup fail to come dripping out of the bottle, eventually. The little kid with the french fries or the grownup with the sizzling grilled burger never felt any anxiety on that score. They knew that ketchup was coming in all its tomatoey goodness.

Some of us have a tendency to pound on the bottom of the bottle or stare up the nozzle, just to be sure that stuff is really inching its way down, but all the while we know that our reward is coming. It is the same when you are operating in the miraculous. You can know for sure that the end you desire is coming, and in fact, the anticipation of the miracle adds to its sweetness. That's why the second key to preparing for a miracle is to anticipate its happening. And remember, have no doubt!

All true believers have a right to expect that these supernatural signs will accompany and confirm their testimony as, in obedience to Christ's command, they seek to proclaim the good news of the gospel to all men.

—DEREK PRINCE
(1915-2003)[1]

To operate in the miraculous, we must anticipate miracles.

Looking again at the miracle beside the temple gate called Beautiful in Acts 3, you will note that there is no hesitation on the part of Peter and John when they see the lame man. They walk up to him and tell him they don't have any money, but what they have they will give. There appears to be no doubt in their minds but that God is about to work a miracle. They don't ask him, "Can we pray with you for healing, brother?" The praying has already been done.

No, they are just expecting God's miraculous response. They anticipated a miracle.

To anticipate means to expect it to happen. The reason you can anticipate or expect success is because God's Word promises it, and you believe the Word. That's one reason I said you should be reading and studying the Bible daily. You must know the Word so you'll know what to expect.

Remember what Jesus told His disciples would be their heritage in Him:

And these signs will follow those who believe: In My name they will cast out demons; they will speak with new tongues; they will take up serpents; and if they drink anything deadly, it will by no means hurt them; they will lay hands on the sick, and they will recover. (Mark 16:17-18)

That's a powerful promise. Add to it this promise from the Lord, "He who believes in Me, the works that I do he will do also; and greater works than these he will do, because I go to My Father. And whatever you ask in My name, that I will do, that the Father may be glorified in the Son" (John 14:12-13).

In these verses, Jesus clearly tells us what to expect, or anticipate. He didn't say, "These signs *may* follow believers." He said they *will* follow us. He didn't say, "My followers *might* do greater works than I have done." He said we *will* do them! You can expect those results because you believe in the Word of God. Remember, to be a disciple Jesus said you must hold to His teaching (John 8:31). Believe God's Word, hold to it, stick to it like glue. We must grab hold of His Word to the point that it becomes a part of us, and we live each moment in anticipation of the next manifestation of the Word.

Peter and John left no room for doubt in their words and actions but that God would heal the lame man. In Mark 9:17-24, we find another situation where a man had a serious problem. His son was tormented almost to the point of death by an evil spirit, and the disciples of Christ couldn't cast it out.

The father cried out to Jesus, "If You can do anything, have compassion on us and help us" (Mark 9:22). Jesus's answer is clear in verse 23: "If *you* can believe, all things are possible to him who believes." In essence Jesus told the man, "The issue is not *if* I can do this, but do you believe I can do this?" There is no question whether Jesus can perform miracles. The only question is whether we believe and anticipate that He will. To operate in the miraculous, we must take Jesus at His word. If He has said He is going to do something, then we must expect that He can and will do what He said.

That's one thing I love about Reinhard Bonnke crusades. He always anticipates the miracle. A year before a crusade, Reinhard Bonnke sends a calendar into every home in the community where the crusade is planned. Thousands of calendars are sent out in hopes that everyone will participate. Of course the only date of significance marked on that calendar is the date of the Reinhard Bonnke crusade, with the time and place and everything laid out. This calendar gets people primed for a glorious time of miracles and healing that is just around the corner. Everyone is planning how to get their sick friends to the crusade to get healed. People walk for miles, dragging themselves there, because they believe their miracle will happen. That calendar helps to create anticipation and build faith for a miracle!

We are seeing this even now at Heartland Fellowship in Dallas/Fort Worth. People are saying, "If I can just get my brother-in-law to church, I know he'll be healed," and, "If I can just get my daughter to church, I know she'll get saved." We've even had people use their cell phone from the back of the church during a service to call their neighbors and say, "Get over here now if you want that touch from God!" They are anticipating miracles.

Are they ever disappointed? Does the miracle they are praying for ever fail to come to pass? Sometimes. Later in this book, we'll discuss why some miracles are delayed or denied. But think about this: in the life of a believer, every miracle of grace that's required does take place.

Let me illustrate. A member of the team helping me prepare this book for publication had a dear friend who had contracted the HIV virus through his actions during his years without God. He then gave his life to Christ, but AIDS was already ravaging his body. Believers began to pray regularly for his miraculous healing, but their prayers were seemingly unheard, and the terrible disease followed its predictable course. After months of decline and heartache, Ben died. Were his friends who had anticipated a miracle wrong in their belief?

Absolutely not, for we know that the moment Ben's broken body breathed its last breath, his eternal soul was released to perfect health and new life with Christ for eternity! He was *more* than healed, he was remade in his heavenly state, never to suffer again, always to be with Jesus, to live forever in the fullness of joy the Bible predicts for us. Who could be disappointed with that outcome?

Anticipation of a miracle is never disappointed, because we know that the outcome of every situation is in God's hands, and however He chooses to handle our struggles will be what is best for us and well worth anticipating.

One way you can create anticipation for a miracle is to talk about Jesus's power to heal and work miracles and to tell the person who needs the miracle, "I'm coming to pray with you tomorrow, so be thinking about that miracle." You get them ready and believing for the miracle. At Heartland, we go ahead and advertise, "If you can get to Heartland on Saturday, you will receive something from God." We create the anticipation for a miracle.

Peter and John could anticipate the miracle at the gate called Beautiful because they had seen their Teacher Jesus do a string of miracles, and they carried in their hearts His promise that they would do even greater things. Christ offers the same promise to you. Anticipate the miracle and you are one step closer to being prepared for operating in the miraculous.

10

KEY #3

Atmosphere

DID YOU EVER ARRIVE FOR A DINNER PARTY at someone's home and right away conclude that your hosts were in the middle of a fight? They don't *say* anything about it, and there's no verbal sparring between husband and wife, but there is just a lot of tension, seemingly in the air itself. It makes you so uncomfortable even to be there because this unfinished business is hanging all around you, although there is no reference to it at all.

Contrast that with the experience of arriving at your daughter's house for dinner to find her glowing and her husband looking delighted. You don't know why, but there's a giddy sense of joy in the air, and then they announce that you are soon to become a grandparent! Even before you knew of the blessed event, you could feel in the air that something wonderful was about to happen.

Atmosphere is something we wander through each moment of the day, but we rarely analyze how we know what the tenor of a situation is. It simply comes to us through human intuition and other ways we cannot quite grasp. There is also an atmosphere for miracles, a situation that allows miraculous operations to thrive. Just as a successful dinner party simply can't happen when both the hosts are glum, a miracle can't happen when there is no atmosphere of faith to believe for it.

That's why the third key to preparing for your miracle is simply to create and enhance the atmosphere where it can happen.

To operate in the miraculous, we must create the atmosphere for a miracle.

The atmosphere is the spiritual environment needed for a miracle. To have a miracle, you must raise the expectation in your own heart and in those around you. Miracles occur when the atmosphere for them is right. Two ingredients must be present for a miracle to take place: need and faith. A miracle is not necessary if there is no need. And, no matter how great the need is, if faith is not present, there will be no atmosphere for miracles.

Remember when Jesus launched His earthly ministry, He quickly grew into a reputation as a miracle worker. Wherever He went, people would run to Him for healing. But when He returned to his hometown of Nazareth and taught in the synagogue, the folks who remembered Him as a kid, the carpenter's son, wouldn't listen to Him. How could He have become such a great teacher? How could He be a worker of miracles? "So they were offended at Him. But Jesus said to them, 'A prophet is not without honor except in his own country and in his own house.' Now He did not do many mighty works there because of their unbelief" (Matthew 13:57-58).

Jesus was constrained from working miracles in Nazareth, not because He didn't want to do them and not because the people didn't need them, but because of the unbelief

Hundreds have been healed just sitting quietly in the audience, without any demonstration whatsoever, and even without admonition… because by His Presence alone, sick bodies are healed.

—KATHRYN KUHLMAN
(1907-1976)[1]

of His neighbors. Although the need for miracles was present, the faith for them was lacking. There was no atmosphere for miracles in Nazareth. No one's heart was open to receive them.

My friend Ernie came into the church office the other day, with his little four-year-old granddaughter. We got to talking, and he told me Madison's mom, his daughter, is a little bitty thing, only about four feet eight, and she never really should have tried to have a baby because she's so tiny. She had a very complicated pregnancy, and when she was about eight months along, she developed pregnancy-induced diabetes and was in terrible pain.

The doctors said her condition was critical, that she might die, that she might lose the baby. And Ernie told me when his daughter was in such pain, he would place his head against her tummy and sing to the baby inside, "I am the Lord that healeth thee..." He created an atmosphere of worship and confidence in God's power to heal, and today mother and daughter are both fine and healthy. And Ernie said one of the first songs Madison could sing the words to as a little baby was the one he had sung to her in the womb, "I am the Lord that healeth thee."

The atmosphere is the final key in preparing for your miracle, and it is one of the most powerful. I remember the first time I attended an open-air crusade in Argentina with the anointed evangelist Carlos Annacondia. He had already won tens of thousands of people to Jesus, and the crowds were just flowing into the service, hungry for God, expecting miracles. The atmosphere just seemed to pulse with the promise of a move of God. Carlos invited me to the stage to give my testimony, and I spoke through an interpreter for about fifteen minutes. When I stepped off the platform and was walking back to my seat, a Gypsy came running up to me. She grabbed my hand, and smacked herself on the head with it, and then she fell out, overcome by the power of God.

When the people around us saw it, more started crowding up to me, and every one I touched started falling under the power. I am ashamed to admit it now, but I was amazed and pleased with myself for this new gift, and I started reaching out and laying hands on everyone! There were some crippled people there wanting prayer, and I touched them and started making my way over to the ambulances which had brought sick people for healing. Then, to my surprise, one of Carlos's assistants ran up to me and told me to stop what I was doing!

I thought, "He doesn't realize how anointed I am right at this minute. I'm on fire!" I tried to explain to him that I was doing stuff I had never seen before. He then sternly spoke to me:

"Yes, but even a child could do what you are doing. Carlos wants you to understand, Steve, that the faith level in this place is so high that anyone who comes to this crusade wanting to be healed is *going* to be healed. And they are so excited, they believe anyone who stands on the platform—even if it's just to make an announcement—is a potential healer. It has nothing to do with you. He wants you to stop because you are disrupting the service."

The atmosphere for a miracle was so strong in that place, even a child could have been healing people left and right. It had nothing to do with me and everything to do with the fact that the need and the faith for a miracle were present so strongly, the atmosphere for the miraculous was there.

We saw the same kind of atmosphere of expectancy during the Brownsville Revival in Pensacola, Florida. This was an extraordinary time when thousands were being saved and healed, and every night the Spirit of God was working powerfully.

A teenage girl who was dying had heard about the revival. One of those foundations that grants the "last request" of dying children offered to make her dream come true before she died, and she asked them to send her to Brownsville to come to church. The foundation has a lot of money, and they had been sending children to Walt Disney World, or overseas, but instead she chose to come to Pensacola to go to a crusade service. Why? Because she had heard there were miracles going on there. She came into the church wearing a baseball cap because her hair had fallen out from the chemotherapy. The atmosphere as always was one of worship, praise, and confidence in God. We prayed for her.

Two weeks later, her father e-mailed us. She had been in for an MRI, and she had not a single tumor growing inside her! Recently my secretary called to check on her, and she's going to a Christian university and has all her hair back. She received God's touch in an atmosphere of healing!

We find this truth evident in all of the crusades led by Pastor Benny Hinn. He is careful to instruct the musicians and singers not to grieve the Holy Spirit. From the very beginning, the music and worship usher in the presence of God. Healings begin to take place because the atmosphere is rich with His healing virtue.

CREATING AN ATMOSPHERE FOR HEALING

How do you create an atmosphere of healing? Look at Peter and John by the gate called Beautiful. The atmosphere there wasn't particularly one for healing—it was more of an atmosphere for begging. That lame man was often there when people passed into the temple, and he was always begging.

The first way Peter and John started to change the atmosphere was with their words. "Look at us," they said (Acts 3:4). The fellow probably didn't look at the people passing by, rather he just raised his hands and cried out for alms. So when the apostles stopped and began talking with him, they were changing his usual routine. They were changing the atmosphere. He looked at them, still hoping for a handout, and right away they changed that idea. "Silver and gold I have none," Peter said, but before the man could protest, he hurried on, "but what I do have, I will give to you" (verse 6).

By their words, the man was moved from an atmosphere of begging to an atmosphere of receiving from God.

EXAMPLES OF NEED MEETING FAITH

The Word is full of other instances where need and faith come together for a miraculous outcome.

Mark 2:1-12 tells a beautiful story of a lame man whose friends tried to bring him to Jesus for healing but found the house too crowded for them to get in. They carried him up to the roof, dug their way down, and lowered the man on a stretcher to the Savior. They had created their own atmosphere for healing, and they weren't taking no for an answer.

Matthew 9:20-22 shares the story of the woman who had been bleeding for twelve years and spent all her money on doctors who couldn't help. But she believed if she could just grab the hem of Jesus's garment, she would be healed. And she was.

Mark 10:46-52 tells the story of Bartimaeus, the blind man who was sitting by the side of the road as Jesus passed by and began to call out to Jesus asking for mercy. The local crowd tried to hush him up, but he just shouted louder. Jesus told him his faith had made him whole and healed him.

In each of these situations, need and faith came together for a miraculous outcome. Without faith, the need can't be met. And without a need, faith isn't necessary. Faith, without doubt, is so important in creating the right atmosphere. Jesus showed us that fact when He removed the mourners and mockers from the room before He raised Jairus's daughter from the dead (Luke 8:49-56). In Acts 9:36-40, Peter also removed the mourners from the room before he raised Tabitha from the dead.

To create the atmosphere for a miracle, sometimes we have to make a concerted effort to remove whatever influences would hinder us from receiving the miracle.

And believe it or not, the atmosphere for a miracle can be created even in the most unlikely of places. I just received a long distance phone call from a staff member, Janet, who had been faithfully praying for her sixteen-year-old brother James's battle with cancer. She called me from his bedside to tell me he had just uttered the words, "I'm going home tonight."

Here many, many believers had been praying for his healing and believing God for his miraculous recovery, but it did not seem to be happening. He was getting worse and had even accepted that he was going to die. But the miraculous thing Janet told me was this: "Pastor, we've been operating in the miraculous all through this time. Many of James's friends have come to the Lord through James's illness. I have been able to pray with them because their hearts were melted by his suffering. We've seen miracles!" The atmosphere for miracles created by those who were praying for James's healing brought his friends to Christ, although it did not result in his physical healing here on earth.

Within an hour of the phone call, James had gone home to be with the Lord. His miracle was completed in heaven. And here, because of his struggle, the prayers generated for his healing had created a perfect atmosphere for miracles, and many of his friends had received spiritual healing and new life in Christ. God wastes nothing, my friend. The dark sorrow of James's family now is cried out in the light of new hope for many of James's friends.

Another unlikely place to create the atmosphere for a miracle is prison. Let's see how two saints in jail created an atmosphere for the miraculous in Acts 16.

Paul and Silas had been preaching in the city of Philippi, where they cast a devil out of a slave girl who had a spirit of divination. The owners of the slave girl were furious because their livelihood was ruined, and they stirred up trouble against Paul and Silas. As a result, the two were severely beaten and thrown into prison. You could say they were in desperate circumstances:

> And when they had laid many stripes on them, they threw them into prison, commanding the jailer to keep them securely. Having received such a charge, he put them into the inner prison and fastened their feet in the stocks. But at midnight Paul and Silas were praying and singing hymns to God, and the prisoners were listening to them. Suddenly there was a great earthquake, so that the foundations of the prison were shaken; and immediately all the doors were opened and everyone's chains were loosed. (Acts 16:23-26)

Look at how Paul and Silas created an atmosphere for a miracle. They had a tremendous need. They needed to be set free from those bonds. But they had a faith that said, "Our God is bigger than these chains. We worship You, Jesus. We love You, Lord. We magnify You in this dungeon. We've never been through anything like this before, but that's okay because You were crucified for us, and You saved us. You took our pain on Yourself when You died for us, Jesus, and we thank You for counting us worthy to suffer for Your name."

Rather than griping and complaining about their chains and looking around at their dark dungeon of despair, they lifted up praise to God and ushered in a life-changing earthquake.

How do you create an atmosphere for a miracle in your home? I can't tell you the number of times my wife, Jeri, and I have received healing by turning our focus away from physical pain and onto the goodness of God. We'll just begin to praise and worship God: "We worship You, Jesus. We praise You for Your presence in this house. We thank You, Lord, that You are the Healer." You can use words to create an atmosphere for miracles in other arenas besides healing.

If you need a financial miracle, you can focus on God's promises of abundance in the Bible, such as Philippians 4:19, "And my God shall supply all your need according to His riches in glory by Christ Jesus." If you want to see your loved ones saved, focus on God's promises of salvation, such as Acts 16:31, "Believe on the Lord Jesus Christ, and you will be saved, you and your household."

Romans 10:17 tells us that faith comes by hearing, and hearing comes by the word of God. We increase our faith by immersing ourselves in the Word. Scripture admonishes us:

- Meditate on the Word—Psalm 1:2
- Speak the Word—Luke 4:4-11
- Pray the Word—John 15:7
- Sing the Word—Psalm 98:1

This is what Paul and Silas did in the Philippian jail, and it is what you can do when you want to create an atmosphere for a miracle by getting your focus off the need and onto the power of God!

Now you know the three keys to preparation for your miracle: authority, anticipation, and atmosphere. You are ready to move on to the three keys to receiving it!

11

KEY #4

Articulation

HAVE YOU EVER BEEN WITH SOMEONE—or worse, behind someone—at the McDonald's drive-through who wasn't ready to order? That's really annoying. They pull right up to the speaker and the conversation goes like this:

"Welcome to McDonald's, may I take your order?"

"Yes...I believe I'll have...the—well, do I want the number one or the number two value meal? I guess make it the...the value meal comes with a drink and fries, right? Okay, well give me the number...one. Or two? One, number one. I think."

"What drink would you like with that?"

"A Coke? No, make it a...Diet Coke. I think, yeah, a Diet Coke. And you know what? Can I have the number two instead of the number one? Yeah, give me the number two value meal, and a Coke."

"Would you like to supersize that?"

"No, no, just—well, I am kinda hungry."

By this time, you're going crazy. *Just order, will ya?!* But the other problem is that the order taker is now just guessing what he really wants—number one or number two? Coke or Diet Coke? Supersized or

Sometimes, while people are struggling… scriptures will come to their minds one after another in answer to their difficulties. Such scriptures are highly pertinent to their circumstances. By this means, their darkness is scattered.

—JONATHAN EDWARDS (1703-1758)[1]

regular? It will be a surprise if he actually receives the right order when he pulls up to the window. That's why my family knows when we pull up to the speaker, they better be able to clearly tell me exactly what they want—and once I begin placing the order, they know better than to interrupt me. I want to place one concise order that is easy for the order taker to understand so we can all get the food we want.

Many kinds of burgers, fries, chicken nuggets, and even salads are available from McDonald's, but there are certain keys to getting what you want from that drive-through window. By the same token, all kinds of supernatural abundance is available from our heavenly Father who loves us and wants to bless us, but there are certain keys to receiving the miracles He intends for us. Earlier, we learned about three keys of preparing for a miracle, and in this chapter, we'll examine the first key to receiving it.

To operate in the miraculous, we must first clearly articulate the miracle. To articulate means to speak distinctly or to express oneself clearly. When you are operating in the miraculous, you not only are speaking your request to God, but you are commanding unseen forces in the spiritual realm, and you must be able to clearly tell them what to do.

Peter and John can again be our example in their dealings with the lame man by the gate called Beautiful. This is all they said to him: "Silver and gold have I none; but such as I have give I thee: In the name of Jesus Christ of Nazareth rise up and walk" (Acts 3:6, KJV). There's no doubt in that sentence what they expected the lame man to do and what they expected to happen to his physical infirmity.

They did not pray over him. They did not tell him if it's God's will and he had faith he would walk. They simply told him to walk.

In fact I would say, unless you have an authentic, and I mean veri-fiable, no-two-ways-about-it Word from God, you should *not* say any more than a very simple instruction such as the one used here. I can't tell you how many wounded families I have seen, how many broken-hearted moms and dads, because some preacher felt led to prophesy a miracle of healing for their little child without actually working the miracle. They prayed over the little one, promised a miracle healing would come, then went on about their business...and the child died. You can't know what that does to a family!

An evangelist friend of mine was telling me about a famous pastor's daughter, who was dying from cancer. If I told you the name, you would know it. Several different ministers said she was going to be healed—one of them even prophesied the *date* she would be healed—but she never received her healing until she went home to be with Jesus.

My friend told me, "Steve, it was an abomination what those men of God did." I agree. They obviously had not heard from the Lord, and although they had faith for the healing, they should never have declared that God had told them the healing would occur or the exact date it would occur. That is ridiculous.

Don't say more than you need to say. Don't make promises for God. That is one kind of authority you don't have unless He makes a special revelation to you. But then, what I am saying is, you make sure you *know* that you *know* the word you have received is from God. A more sure and faithful way to articulate the miracle is to say what you already know to be true from the verifiable evidence of the Bible.

For instance, you can say to God, "God, our brother here is suf-fering from cancer. I know You are a God of miracles, and it is Your desire to heal." You can say to the person, "My Jesus heals, and He is here right now, and I know He can heal you." That is all true, and it builds your faith as well as the faith of the person who needs the miracle. Then you can speak to the cancer, "I rebuke that cancer in Jesus's name." It's all very straightforward.

Another way to articulate the need for a healing miracle that builds faith in you and in the person in need is to use a scripture that reflects

God's power to heal. This leaves no doubt about what you are asking God to do and what response you expect in the physical realm to your spiritual petition. Here are some scriptures that are easy to memorize and are full of God's power regarding healing:

- "I am the LORD who heals you" (Exodus 15:26).
- "So you shall serve the LORD your God, and He will bless your bread and your water. And I will take sickness away from the midst of you" (Exodus 23:25).
- "Who forgives all your iniquities, who heals all your diseases" (Psalm 103:3).
- "But He was wounded for our transgressions, He was bruised for our iniquities; the chastisement for our peace was upon Him, and by His stripes we are healed" (Isaiah 53:5).
- "Jesus Christ is the same yesterday, today, and forever" (Hebrews 13:8).
- "And the prayer of faith will save the sick, and the Lord will raise him up. And if he has committed sins, he will be forgiven" (James 5:15).

Speak these scriptures aloud and with confidence, for they are your heritage as a believer, and you have the authority of Jesus to claim their promise. You can also speak healing directly to the person in need, as Jesus did in John 5:8: "Rise, take up your bed and walk." He also raised a dead man with a simple command: "Lazarus, come forth" (John 11:43). A simple "Be healed in the name of Jesus Christ" has all the authority of God's kingdom, and it clearly articulates so there is no doubt in all the spirit world of what you intend to happen.

You do not need to sound like a preacher and pray a lengthy prayer in the King James Version to get God's attention or to impress the person in need of a miracle. That is not necessary and not biblical. When you look at the miracles of the New Testament saints, they were done in a very matter-of-fact way, short and to the point. Jesus raised Jairus's daughter from the dead with the simple words, "Little girl, I say to you, arise" (Mark 5:41).

It's also appropriate for you to approach the person in need with assurance that God desires to heal. You are not going to offend your heavenly Father by asking Him to do something He has already promised to do and has already shown you that He is more than willing and more than able to do.

You don't have to pray some generic prayer that gives God a lot of outs, just in case He doesn't feel like healing today: "God, if it be Your will for healing to restore this person's body in this physical world, then we ask for Your perfect solution to this situation that confronts us." What does that even mean? What on earth are you asking for? The spiritual forces of hell just laugh at a prayer like that, because it is full of holes. It is the prayer of someone who has no authority but is vainly hoping God might surprise Him with a miracle. Don't bother with that.

If that is how you truly feel, that you have no power for a miracle, then instead of praying a wishy-washy prayer like that, which gives God no clue as to what you're really after, I suggest you go back to the beginning of this book and start again. Only this time, where I have listed some of the many "commonplace" miracles of the Bible, take your Bible and read the whole story, verse by verse.

Ask God to reveal to you as you read the awesome power that underlies every verse. When you come to the miracles of the New Testament, ask God to reveal to you the awesome love that was His motivating factor in all the miracles of healing and deliverance. And then reread the Gospels and pay attention to every miracle of Jesus, thinking about the reasons He performed each one.

As you read through these miracles and pray for God to reveal Himself through His Word, I believe it is going to build your faith so that you will realize this: you are a joint heir with Jesus, you have received His authority to work miracles in order to further His kingdom, and He wants to express His awesome love in action for a lost world *through you*. Then, the next time you pray for a miracle, you won't feel like you have to pray some mamby-pamby prayer that might or might not get answered. You will understand that as a child of the King, you can come boldly to the throne of grace and speak straightforward of your miracle need (Hebrews 4:16)!

Am I saying that God will always answer your prayer with a miracle? Obviously not. There are many times I pray for a miracle and do not receive one. In fact, later in this book we'll discuss the ABCs of delayed or denied miracles for reasons why you may not have received your miracle yet. What I *am* saying is that God is well able to perform a miracle, and you do not need to hold back in your prayers of faith on His account.

You don't have to offer God a vague prayer so He can save face if He doesn't deliver a miracle. You don't have to offer God a lengthy prayer with a lot of big spiritual words in it—He understands plain English. All you have to do is speak clearly and boldly the action you desire in the name of Jesus. This is how the saints of old articulated miracles, and you can do the same.

If you personally need healing, you can clearly articulate what God's Word says about your need, and then speak that healing into existence in the name of Jesus. If you need provision, boldly declare what God has said in His Word about providing for your needs, then speak that provision into existence. Just say it: "I speak God's power to provide for me over this economic situation in the name of Jesus Christ." When you have mastered the keys for operating in the miraculous, it's true that there is a miracle in your mouth!

12

KEY #5

Administration

ONCE THERE WAS A GUY who was swept away by the idea of the Day-Timer. He had heard so much about Day-Timers! People who had begun using Day-Timers told him they had so much more time now that they were better organized.

He found out from a Day-Timer seminar that once he possessed a Day-Timer of his own, he would never miss another meeting, never forget another important idea, always know when he was supposed to be where and how much time he had to meet his pressing deadlines. His friends said the Day-Timer had revolutionized their workdays, freed up their weekends to spend time with their families, given them better focus on their jobs.

He could hardly fathom how a little thing like a notebook planner could do so much for him, but he was eager to give it a try. He bought the Day-Timer, took it to work, and flung it on top of the mess of his disorganized files. Then he waited for the miraculous transformation from scraps of paper and lost agendas to a place for everything and everything in its place. After two weeks, he angrily threw the Day-Timer away. It had not done a single thing for him except sit there on top of the mess!

I instructed them about healing and prayed for them to be healed... then I asked them to put their faith into action, to begin to do what they couldn't do before the prayer....
It seemed that the healing power of God literally exploded across the field....
It would take a great book to begin to recount the wonders of God wrought this night.
—T. L. OSBORN[1]

A miracle is kind of like the Day-Timer or any other modern-day organizational tool. It has an incredible power to make a difference, but it takes an action on your part to release that power. That's why you have to learn how to administrate the miracle.

To operate in the miraculous, we must be willing to administrate the miracle. That merely means we must manage it, or take charge of it. This is where we believers can sometimes make a mistake, because every miracle is unique, and every miracle has its own fingerprint. There is no one-size-fits-all method for administration of the miracle. The way God heals one time might not be the way He does it the next time. That's also the exciting part about administrating the miracle, because we have to listen for God's voice and use the wisdom He gives us.

By the temple gate Beautiful, Peter and John administrated the miracle by speaking healing over the lame man, but they went a step further. Peter commanded him to rise and walk, then "he took him by the right hand and lifted him up, and immediately his feet and ankle bones received strength" (Acts 3:7). Although Peter's words to the man had been full of faith, the miracle of healing did not occur until Peter reached out to help the man up. Often, the miracle occurs only when the administration portion of the event has begun.

In another example Jesus healed Peter's mother-in-law. The scripture says, "So He touched her hand, and the fever left her"

(Matthew 8:15). This healing required a touch. Matthew 9 tells of Jesus's healing some blind men: "Then He touched their eyes, saying, 'According to your faith let it be to you.' And their eyes were opened" (9:29-30). Another time Jesus healed a blind man by rubbing His own spit on the man's eyes (Mark 8:22-25). He enabled Peter to walk on water simply by calling the disciple to come to Him (Matthew 14:28-32). There is always an action required when administrating a miracle.

Several years ago I was diagnosed with a serious blood disease that my doctor told me was fatal. There was a treatment that was effective in 5 percent of the cases, but the side effects were brutal, and it didn't seem to be worth the slim hope it offered. I believed God would heal me, and I only told my wife and a few close friends about the terrible diagnosis. But halfway around the world, God spoke to a wonderful believer named Suzette Hattingh, one of the greatest prayer warriors I have ever known. She had worked with Reinhard Bonnke for many years as his chief intercessor. God revealed to her that I was very sick, and she began to pray for me.

She then felt led to fly to Pensacola, Florida, where I was. She came into my office and said, "God spoke to me that you are seriously sick, and I want to pray for you!" She spoke with such authority, not saying, "You are healed," but she did say, "Stephen, I'm believing God to heal you right now." We prayed together, and then she said, "Now you have to go back to the doctor and have him redo those blood tests." That was Suzette administrating the miracle. It wasn't enough for her to pray and speak healing over me; she had to give me that final instruction: go back to the doctor.

You may be thinking, "Steve, why was that important? Weren't you already healed?" That's the beauty of this key to receiving your miracle: you never know what God is going to do or how He is going to do it! Remember when Jesus healed the ten lepers? "He said to them, 'Go, show yourselves to the priests.' And so it was that as they went, they were cleansed" (Luke 17:14). Leprosy was such a contagious and debilitating disease that anyone who had it was put out of society, and the only way to be reinstated was to prove to the priest that you had been cleansed, healed. Jesus told them to take it by faith that they were healed and go right to the priest. And the Scriptures say as they went they received their healing! Every miracle is different, and each one is going to be administered differently.

When Suzette told me to go back to the doctor, I went. I requested another set of blood tests, and they came back completely clean. No trace of that fatal disease! Perplexed, the doctors wanted to run the tests again, so I took them a third time, and again the results came back to show I was completely healthy.

Suzette administrated the miracle in the way God showed her. In effect she said, "That disease is going, in the name of Jesus, and then let's get proof from the medical profession of your divine healing so we can show people just what our God can do!"

In the same way, Jesus and the disciples often administrated miracles by asking the person to do something they couldn't do before in order to demonstrate God's healing power. Jesus healed a man with a withered hand in Matthew 12:13: "Then He said to the man, 'Stretch out your hand.' And he stretched it out, and it was restored as whole as the other." Before, he couldn't stretch out his withered hand, but at Jesus's word he could, and did. You too can administrate miracles by simply asking the person to do what they couldn't do before.

Do *not*, unless you receive some very specific, authentic, and undeniable insight from God, go pulling anyone up out of their wheelchair or taking away their cane or walker. You are not a doctor, nor are you omniscient to know exactly what has taken place, so you do not want to force someone to do something that might injure them further.

In Argentina, we were privileged to see many handicapped people completely healed by God, but I did not grab them and pull them out of their wheelchairs. I just told them to do something that they couldn't do before. If they couldn't stand before and they had been healed, they would jump up on their own. I saw this happen many times, but I have also met many people who are paralyzed who don't even *want* anyone to pray for them anymore because the last time some overzealous believer prayed for them, he jerked them out of their chair and embarrassed them.

Put yourself in the place of the paraplegic who has not felt God's touch yet is pulled out of her chair by the evangelist who is forcing her to stand on wobbling feet. The evangelist then commences to praise God for the healing. She knows she's not healed, and all she wants to do is sit back down in her chair. It's humiliating for her and for the preacher who thinks she's healed. So when you are praying for someone's healing, you must administrate the miracle, but you must *not* make a spectacle of it or physically force the person to take some action.

Now you know how to articulate the miracle and how to administrate the miracle. The final key is this: how to advertise the Miracle Worker.

13

KEY #6

Advertising

ADVERTISING MIRACLES SOUNDS TOO MADISON AVENUE for you, right? Miracles are a big spiritual deal, and the last thing they need are some kind of carnal-minded public relations campaign. You think?

The way I read my Bible, God was the first and best advertising executive. After all, He originated the best advertising strategy in the world: the free sample: "Oh, taste and see that the LORD is good" (Psalm 34:8). Do you ever walk by the Godiva Chocolatier store in the mall and one of the employees hands you a free truffle? A truffle is usually deep dark or milk chocolate wrapped around some kind of luscious soft center. You take one bite, and you want to take a pound home for later. That's advertising. "Taste and see" is God's advertising campaign.

Look at Jesus for another example of how He made Himself known. He met a woman at the well, and asked her for a drink. She was surprised that a Hebrew man would speak to her, much less drink from her bucket. And He said, "Whoever drinks of this water will thirst again, but whoever drinks of the water that I shall give him will never thirst" (John 4:13-14).

Jesus didn't even have His own bucket. He didn't have a single drop of physical water to give this woman, but He captured her attention by

The Lord is the great promoter of divine possibility, pressing you into the attitude of daring to believe all the Word says. We are to be living words, epistles of Christ, known and read of all men.

—SMITH WIGGLESWORTH (1859-1947)[1]

promising something that she really wanted: water that would allow her never to thirst again.

Jesus knew what the woman most wanted and promised it to her to get her interested in what He had to say so He could give her what she most *needed.* The idea of living water...what a great form of advertising! God has assigned you an advertising campaign of your own, and it is the third key to receiving your miracle.

To operate in the miraculous, we must be willing to advertise Jesus the Miracle Worker. Jesus's many miracles of healing were events that He used to advertise the power of His Father, such as this one in Matthew 9:2-8:

> Then behold, they brought to Him a paralytic lying on a bed. When Jesus saw their faith, He said to the paralytic, "Son, be of good cheer; your sins are forgiven you."
>
> And at once some of the scribes said within themselves, "This Man blasphemes!"
>
> But Jesus, knowing their thoughts, said, "Why do you think evil in your hearts? For which is easier, to say, 'Your sins are forgiven you,' or to say, 'Arise and walk'? But that you may know that the Son of Man has power on earth to forgive sins"—then He said to the paralytic, "Arise, take up your bed, and go to your house." And he arose and departed to his house.
>
> Now when the multitudes saw it, they marveled and glorified God, who had given such power to men.

This miracle was a vehicle of advertising Jesus the Miracle Worker in several ways. First, Jesus established His authority to forgive sins by performing a miracle that proved His power. Secondly, Jesus saw to it that when the crowd of witnesses began to marvel, they "glorified God who had given such power." Jesus intended for this miracle to reflect on the power of the Father, just as the miracles Jesus grants us today are intended to glorify Him and advertise His power.

So don't discount the idea that part of receiving a miracle is learning to *advertise* the Miracle Worker.

In fact, the miracle itself is just another way that God advertises the glory of His Son to draw the lost to Him. The healing of the lame man beside the gate called Beautiful caused such a disturbance, Peter and John were quickly surrounded by a crowd of people who wanted to see what all the commotion was about. The disciples—and the formerly lame man—had become a walking advertisement for Jesus. And the first thing the apostles did after they were used by the Lord to heal the lame man was to turn all of the attention away from themselves and give the glory for this miracle to Jesus. Look at Acts 3:11-16:

> Now as the lame man who was healed held on to Peter and John, all the people ran together to them in the porch which is called Solomon's, greatly amazed. So when Peter saw it, he responded to the people: "Men of Israel, why do you marvel at this? Or why look so intently at us, as though by our own power or godliness we had made this man walk? The God of Abraham, Isaac, and Jacob, the God of our fathers, glorified His Servant Jesus, whom you delivered up and denied in the presence of Pilate, when he was determined to let Him go. But you denied the Holy One and the Just, and asked for a murderer to be granted to you, and killed the Prince of life, whom God raised from the dead, of which we are witnesses. And His name, through faith in His name, has made this man strong, whom you see and know. Yes, the faith which comes through Him has given him this perfect soundness in the presence of you all."

Peter and John glorified Jesus as they boldly declared that Christ was the One who healed the man. Not only were they a walking advertisement, but they seized the moment and preached Christ to the multitude.

When you begin operating in the miraculous, you may be tempted to say to yourself, "I must be something special for God to use me like this!" The minute you begin thinking that way, you lose your focus on advertising the Miracle Worker—Jesus—and begin to focus on advertising the tool, which is you. If you start thinking you are the big-deal miracle worker yourself, you are mistaken. That would be like a scalpel declaring itself a brilliant surgeon. The doctor is the one who wields the scalpel. You are just the tool the Lord uses to perform mighty works, and He expects you to reflect the glory back to Him.

In Acts 14, Paul had the perfect setup to start seizing some of that miracle glory for himself. He and Barnabas were preaching in the city of Lystra when they saw a crippled man. The Holy Spirit must have spoken to Paul that this man had the faith to be healed, and Paul said to him, "Stand up straight on your feet!" (Acts 14:10). The Bible says the man leaped and walked!

The next thing you know, the inhabitants of Lystra declared Paul and Barnabas to be the gods Mercury and Jupiter and brought flowers and oxen to sacrifice to them. The priest of Zeus thought his pagan gods had come to preach to them. What was Paul and Barnabas's response to this warm welcome from the pagan priest and all the people? They tore their clothes in despair and cried out:

> Men, why are you doing these things? We also are men with the same nature as you, and preach to you that you should turn from these useless things to the living God, who made the heaven, the earth, the sea, and all things that are in them, who in bygone generations allowed all nations to walk in their own ways. Nevertheless He did not leave Himself without witness, in that He did good, gave us rain from heaven and fruitful seasons, filling our hearts with food and gladness. (Acts 14:15-17)

Paul immediately gave the glory to God, and redirected the focus of the crowd to Jesus, again preaching Christ to the multitude. It's obvious that one of God's primary purposes in performing signs and wonders is to glorify Jesus and disperse the message of salvation to the greatest number of people.

In Matthew 9:32-33 we read about Jesus, just after He had healed two blind men: "As they went out, behold, they brought to Him a man, mute and demon-possessed. And when the demon was cast out, the mute spoke. And the multitudes marveled, saying, 'It was never seen like this in Israel!'" Christ's acts of compassion and healing spurred another most effective advertising technique: word-of-mouth testimony. Multitudes marveled!

I think about a Tarrant County, Texas, deputy named Raymond at our church, Heartland Fellowship. All Raymond's friends and neighbors knew that he was heading for a crisis in his life because of complications from a kidney transplant. For three-quarters of a year, he'd been forced to wear an orthopedic boot and brace, from the moment he got out of bed in the morning until he got back in bed at night, to prevent a creeping fracture from moving up his leg.

The doctors said if they couldn't stop it, he would be forced to undergo surgery to fuse the bone from his ankle all the way up his leg. When that happened, it was possible he would have to give up his active job as a law-enforcement officer. In the meantime, Raymond was in terrible pain, and it took all his strength just to do his job each day, come home, and collapse. All his friends and neighbors knew about his health problems and for months had seen him in his brace. Someone invited him to our small-group Bible study that was focusing on the very topic you're reading about now: operating in the miraculous. That night the group prayed for Raymond.

Two weeks later the throbbing pain in his foot disappeared! Raymond was so encouraged that he did something he hadn't done in nine months: he wore his regular shoes instead of his special boot and brace. Previously, he *couldn't* put his regular shoes on because of the swelling and pain. That day, he was able to walk around the house in his regular shoes with no pain. Next, he took his dog and his granddaughter for a walk around the neighborhood—still no swelling, no pain.

The next day Raymond wore his old work shoes to work, and he came home that evening for the first time in months with energy to spare! Since then he has never again worn his brace, and his leg is completely well.

Naturally, Raymond was excited about what happened to him, and he became a walking advertisement of operating in the miraculous. All his friends were overwhelmed by his recovery, and Raymond told them all that the Miracle Worker Jesus had made it possible. One friend, who was hospitalized with cancer, had just been sent home by the doctors who had given up on him. They said there was nothing more they could do, and the man would be more comfortable dying at home.

Raymond's testimony inspired the man to trust Jesus for his healing, and today that man's condition is improving by leaps and bounds. He went home to die, but instead he's a testimony to God's power.

A firsthand witness of God's miracle-working power makes all the difference. When you *read* about a new product, you might be mildly interested to try it out, but when your neighbor starts telling you that he tried it and it's the best thing since sliced bread, then you get excited about trying it for yourself! He has no reason to lie to you, no stake in getting you to try the product; he's just excited about what a great thing it is. That is the best possible advertising.

Are you ready to wear a signboard for Jesus, to become a walking advertisement of His glory as Paul and the other apostles did? You can begin right now. You don't have to wait for some miracle of healing or deliverance to be worked through you, because you have already experienced a miracle: your salvation.

It's been said that the person with an experience is never at the mercy of the person with an argument. That means if you have experienced something incredible, no one can persuade you that it wasn't. Every person who has been born again has experienced something incredible—the new birth: "Thanks be to God for His indescribable gift" (2 Corinthians 9:15). What a miracle it is when a life that was dead in sin, separated from God and destined for eternity in hell, receives the forgiveness of sin and is born again as a child of God! The Bible says those who are in Christ are a new creation. Old things have passed away, and everything has become new (2 Corinthians 5:17).

ADVERTISE THE MIRACLE WORKER

You have experienced that miracle, and you can be advertising the Miracle Worker. Start right where you are. Begin to tell people what God has done in your life. He has forgiven you. He has changed your life. He has blessed you. He has provided for your needs. He has answered your prayers. He has given you a new song. He has given you peace of mind.

If you have any experience with marketing, you know that one important facet of your campaign is to have a slogan, a catchphrase that people can latch on to. You can easily memorize many important slogans from the Bible that will help you advertise the Miracle Worker in your life. Here are a few ideas just for starters:

- "For all have sinned and fall short of the glory of God" (Romans 3:23).
- "For the wages of sin is death, but the gift of God is eternal life in Christ Jesus our Lord" (Romans 6:23).
- "If you confess with your mouth the Lord Jesus and believe in your heart that God has raised Him from the dead, you will be saved. For with the heart one believes unto righteousness, and with the mouth confession is made unto salvation" (Romans 10:9-10).
- "For God so loved the world that He gave His only begotten Son, that whoever believes in Him should not perish but have everlasting life" (John 3:16).
- "If we confess our sins, He is faithful and just to forgive us our sins and to cleanse us from all unrighteousness" (1 John 1:9).
- "As far as the east is from the west, so far has He removed our transgressions from us" (Psalm 103:12).

In these scriptures is the encapsulated essence of what Jesus did for us when He saved us from our sins, and that is a miracle of which every believer can speak with confidence. And here is another great thing. As you begin to speak of God's goodness and advertise what the Miracle Worker has already done for you, you will create an atmosphere for miracles and an anticipation of miracles so that more miracles will come your way!

If you have mastered the keys to preparing for and receiving your miracle, if you have faith to operate in the miraculous, and yet for some reason you have still not received your miracle, hold on. In these next chapters, we'll examine why some miracles are delayed or even denied. You may be surprised at the answers.

THE ABCs *of* WHY SOME MIRACLES ARE DELAYED *or* DENIED

THIS FINAL SECTION OF OUR STUDY is a focus on some of the reasons why miracles are delayed or why they don't manifest at all. Remember, God intends for His children to operate in the miraculous on a normal basis, just as the first-century Christians did. Is there something wrong with us when miracles don't happen? No, there's no blame when a miracle doesn't happen. But there is probably an explanation.

In the following chapters, we'll examine the age-old question, Why are some people healed and others are not? Or for those who need a miracle other than physical healing, Where is *my* miracle? Let me tell you my definitive answer to those questions: *I don't know.* Our God is omniscient, and only He knows for sure. He is sovereign. That means He is the One who possesses undisputed, supreme authority, power, and knowledge. Until He tells us face to face what His reasoning was—if He ever tells us, if we even care once we see Him face to face—we may never know the answers.

If God, for whatever reason, did give us an explanation, who is to say we would understand it? We are a little grain of sand on the beach, but God created the beach. If you've ever been to my church, perhaps you have heard me say, "Big God. Little me." That is a statement that I often find myself quoting when I don't understand what is going on. It may be that we just aren't equipped to understand God's purposes. "For My thoughts are not your thoughts, nor are your ways My ways, says the LORD. For as the heavens are higher than the earth, so are My ways higher than your ways, and My thoughts than your thoughts" (Isaiah 55:8-9).

Think of it this way. When your child asks you why she can't live at Walt Disney World every day, your answer is something like this: "Well, honey, you have to pay money to get into Disney World, and Daddy gets his money by going to work every day in Dallas, so if we moved here to Disney World, we would run out of money, and then they wouldn't let us go in anymore." How much of that do you think a four-year-old understands? All she knows is that she wants to live at Disney World, and you are saying no. You're doing your best with the simplest answer you can think of, but she doesn't really get it.

That's sort of how it is with you and me asking God why we can't have our miracle. There is a good reason, and He would like us to understand it, but maybe we're just not capable of understanding it.

That said, this teaching is not to be viewed as an excuse for why some miracles do not happen, because I do not know why. Nor is it a list of reasons why you shouldn't trust God for a miracle, because we know that He wants us to have miracles in our lives.

We know this from the Word of God itself. It is certain that God wants to heal our bodies (Exodus 15:26). It is certain that God wants us to prosper in all areas of our lives (Jeremiah 29:11). It is certain God wants our loved ones to be saved (2 Peter 3:9). The list of the blessings God wants us to enjoy in this life goes on and on.

And we know that each miracle consists of two parts: God's power and man's faith. Psalm 103:3 says God is the One "who forgives all your iniquities, who heals all your diseases." That's God's part. Man's part is found in Jesus's words: "Therefore I say to you, whatever things you ask when you pray, believe that you receive them, and you will have them" (Mark 11:24).

There is God's part and man's part, but somewhere in the middle between the two is where things can get murky. This is the area we'll be exploring—the ABCs of why a miracle may be delayed or even denied.

14

Reason #1

A Is for Agenda

There are times when God does not perform a miracle because His agenda is not the same as ours.

An agenda is a list of tasks to be accomplished, usually according to a time-related schedule. Have you noticed all the new gadgets and systems designed to keep people on their agenda these days? Everyone is becoming more and more focused on spending their time as productively as possible, and they are keeping track of every moment.

First it was the Day-Timer—that's the first big organizational system I remember. It suggests you write down every appointment, every goal for every meeting, every deadline with reminders in advance. It's a great system! But then came Franklin Covey with the What Matters Most system. Some like it better because it is a holistic program that starts with the things you value most in life and the goals you hope to achieve in this lifetime, then it helps you build your daily schedule around that. What could be better?

The Covey program for your PDA! For the less computer conversant, that's a personal digital assistant—a handheld computer. They have names like BlackBerry, PalmPilot, and iPAQ, and allow the user to send

What may not one man do in a brief life, if he is willing to be simply a living conduit-pipe through which the power of God may descend to men? There is no limit to the possible usefulness of such a life.
—F. B. MEYER
(1847-1929)[1]

and receive e-mail, store important data, interface with a base computer, and now organize your entire life with What Matters Most or another scheduling system.

With these calendars and devices, people can organize their whole day into fifteen-minute increments and schedule their achievements in career and family development about twenty years down the road. We can set our agenda for the next two decades!

God, too, has a plan and schedule, and often His agenda doesn't coincide with ours. The classic example of this in the New Testament is Jesus's allowing His good friend Lazarus to die from an illness, when the Savior Himself was just a few miles away and could easily have come to Lazarus's aid. We have examined some different aspects of this story in earlier chapters, and now we will consider it in light of God's agenda.

There is no doubt that Jesus loved Lazarus and wanted him to live. When Mary and Martha sent for the Savior, their message told him, "The one You love is sick." There was no question that Lazarus was a dear friend. There was also no doubt that Jesus could have healed Lazarus. He had been going about healing every Tom, Dick, and Larry who asked for help, and these were people who were not close friends as Lazarus was.

To you and me—and incidentally to Lazarus's sisters, Mary and Martha—it made no sense that when Jesus received word that His friend was ill, He did not immediately hurry to Bethany to heal him. Martha even told Jesus when He finally arrived, "Lord, if You had been here, my brother would not have died" (John 11:21).

What was so important to Jesus that He tarried for two days after learning of Lazarus's illness? The Bible doesn't say. It just says He stayed where He was for two more days. That's how important it was. And it wasn't as if Jesus didn't know Lazarus was likely to die. In fact, He knew that Lazarus *had* died before He ever started out for Bethany. "Then Jesus said to them plainly, 'Lazarus is dead. And I am glad for your sakes that I was not there, that you may believe. Nevertheless let us go to him'" (John 11:14).

Now to the disciples, that made no sense. Earlier, Jesus had narrowly avoided being stoned to death in Judea, and the disciples clearly did not think it was a good idea to return to such a climate. Still, I am sure they felt it was worth the risk if Jesus could save the life of their friend Lazarus, but when Jesus told them Lazarus was already dead…well, hold up. Why go into territory You know is hostile to You if there's no hope of healing Lazarus?

The disciples had their agenda, and it seemed to be freeing the nation of Israel from the Roman tyranny. They wanted Jesus to be a conquering King and Messiah—something that couldn't happen if He walked into some kind of trap in Bethany. Nevertheless, to their credit, the disciples didn't balk. Thomas said to the others, "Let us also go, that we may die with Him" (John 11:16). Although the whole program made no sense to them, the disciples went along because of their love for Jesus and their faith in Him.

Martha and Mary had their agenda, too. They simply wanted their brother healed and restored to them. But Jesus delayed His coming and Lazarus died. When He finally showed up on the scene several days after Lazarus had died, Martha and Mary were heartbroken. In her pain, Martha rebuked Jesus saying, "Lord, if You had been here, my brother would not have died" (John 11:21), or, "Jesus, where's our miracle?"

So why *did* Jesus let Lazarus die? The answer is quite obvious. Because He wanted people to see His power. Raising Lazarus from the dead was a *big* miracle—much bigger than if Jesus had simply healed Lazarus. Look at what happened as a result:

Then Jesus, again groaning in Himself, came to the tomb. It was a cave, and a stone lay against it. Jesus said, "Take away the stone."

Martha, the sister of him who was dead, said to Him, "Lord, by this time there is a stench, for he has been dead four days."

Jesus said to her, "Did I not say to you that if you would believe you would see the glory of God?" Then they took away the stone from the place where the dead man was lying. And Jesus lifted up His eyes and said, "Father, I thank You that You have heard Me. And I know that You always hear Me, but because of the people who are standing by I said this, that they may believe that You sent Me." Now when He had said these things, He cried with a loud voice, "Lazarus, come forth!" And he who had died came out bound hand and foot with grave clothes, and his face was wrapped with a cloth. Jesus said to them, "Loose him, and let him go."

Then many of the Jews who had come to Mary, and had seen the things Jesus did, believed in Him. (John 11:38-45, emphasis added)

Remember, God's agenda always includes souls. Because Jesus raised Lazarus from the dead, many of the Jews believed in Him.

There are several interesting things about this passage that reflect on the idea of God's agenda being different from ours. First, Jesus makes clear to all that this miracle is different from others, because He had deliberately staged it to glorify God and prove to the skeptics that He was sent from God and was God "that they may believe that You sent Me." This explains exactly why He waited so long to come to Lazarus's rescue. But there was more. Remember I told you every miracle is about souls? This one was one of the most important in that regard.

I believe Jesus knew that not everyone would be happy about His miracle. Look at John 11:46-47:

But some of them went away to the Pharisees and told them the things Jesus did. Then the chief priests and the Pharisees gathered a council and said, "What shall we do? For this Man works many signs. If we let Him alone like this, everyone will believe in Him, and the Romans will come and take away both our place and nation."

It was right here that they first hatched their plot to kill Jesus. Perhaps Jesus knew that this would be the end result of raising Lazarus from the dead, and at least part of His tears and groaning were caused by the knowledge that He was setting in motion the horrible torture and humiliation that He had to face in order to save us. Yes, He came to take His place as the Lamb of God who would take away the sins of the world, but knowing the agenda ahead of time did not necessarily make it any easier for Him.

He suffered unimaginable torture and agony as He willingly bore our sins and carried our pains on that cross. Revelation 13:8 speaks of Jesus as "the Lamb, slain from the foundation of the world." Think about it. Before the world was ever created, God's agenda was that Jesus would die for the sins of the world so that we could be born again. This was the Father's agenda, and this was Jesus's agenda. He willingly laid down His life for us and for the will of the Father.

What a Savior. What a God!

Some believe that the miracle of Jesus's raising Lazarus from the dead set in motion the devastating chain of events that would culminate in His death. But that was God's agenda. Mary and Martha's agenda, the disciples' agenda, your agenda, and mine...those don't matter much when it comes to the *real* agenda. God sees the big picture. We see just a portion. He sees everything clearly. We see only in part (1 Corinthians 13:12). He doesn't move in the exact way we ask sometimes because He has a bigger goal than we can imagine.

Mary and Martha saw the goal of having their dear brother restored to them, and to them that was a huge goal. Jesus saw the very essence of His objective in coming to earth: the fulfillment of messianic prophecy. He saw His death on the cross and our salvation, and that was a much, much bigger goal.

Sometimes our goals get swallowed up in His goals. But when our prayers and our agenda line up with His purposes, we position ourselves to receive His miracles.

15

REASON #2

B Is for Belief

THERE ARE TIMES THAT GOD DOES NOT PERFORM A MIRACLE because He wants to strengthen our belief.

If you ever had a wild child who got away from the Lord as a teenager and went downhill from there, you may have been plagued with unbelief. Although you want desperately to see that young man restored and back in fellowship with God, you don't really believe it can happen because of all you've been through with his rebellion. You may come to me and ask me to pray for the salvation of Billy Bob. I'll ask you what Billy Bob's spiritual state is right now, and you'll list a litany of ways he has gone wrong: "He's a divorced alcoholic who won't pay his child support and lives in sin with some woman, making a living off the government by faking disability, and on top of that, he owes me seventeen thousand dollars. He's rotten to the core, and I don't see how he'll ever get saved."

To me, the person you're describing is somebody primed and ready to come to Jesus. I mean, I was dying from years of drug abuse when I came to Christ, so what's a little old case of alcoholism and immorality to me? I can pray the prayer of faith with the assurance that God is listening. I can visualize that Billy Bob is right on the verge of experiencing a life transformation. Why? Because I've been there, and I know that God can do it again.

It may be a little more difficult for you because you've had to live with Billy Bob all these years and experience every heartache he has caused. You've had to post his bail, buy his kids' clothes, sober him up after a weekend binge. You know your grown child is a scumbucket;

If all believers do not in fact have these gifts in operation, it is not because God withholds them but simply because such believers through ignorance or carelessness or unbelief fail to press on into the fullness of God's revealed will for His people.

—DEREK PRINCE
(1915-2003)[1]

it's very depressing, and you can't think of anything that is going to change his ways.

That's human nature. But God wants you to trust Him for Billy Bob's salvation no matter how hopeless the situation looks for no other reason except that He made a promise to you.

The Bible says faith is "the substance of things hoped for, the evidence of things not seen" (Hebrews 11:1). If you had all kinds of evidence that Billy Bob was just about to get saved, you wouldn't need any faith at all. You could just believe your eyes. But in the absence of any indication that Billy Bob will ever turn his life around, it takes a great amount of pure faith to keep on believing. That is the kind of belief God wants you to develop.

This, then, can be seen as the next factor in why some miracles are delayed or denied: There are times when God does not perform a miracle because our belief in Him is weak and needs to be strengthened.

There are only a few cases in the Bible where the scripture notes that God did *not* perform a miracle. One of them discussed earlier was in Matthew 13, where Jesus came to preach in His hometown, and nobody would give Him any respect because they had known Him growing up, remembered Him from back then, and didn't see how that brainy little boy that used to play with their sons could now be some big-shot rabbi.

> When He had come to His own country, He taught them in their synagogue, so that they were astonished and said, "Where did this Man get this wisdom and these mighty works? Is this not the carpenter's son? Is not His mother called Mary? And His brothers James, Joses, Simon, and Judas? And His sisters, are they not all with us? Where then did this Man get all these things?" So they were offended at Him. But Jesus said to them, "A prophet is not without honor except in his own country and in his own house." Now He did not do many mighty works there because of their unbelief. (Matthew 13:54-58)

Why was it that Jesus could not work miracles in His hometown? Because of the unbelief of the people. What did their unbelief stem from? Their history with Jesus. They could not set aside what they knew about Him as the carpenter's son and believe that He had miraculous powers, much the same way you may be finding it difficult to set aside your history with Billy Bob and believe that God can change him. To build and strengthen your faith, God may be waiting on your miracle until you can set the past aside and believe wholly on Him.

Another biblical record of a miracle *not* happening is in Matthew 17 when the disciples couldn't cast out a demon. It is interesting because the disciples had healed the sick and cast out demons before, so why should their faith fail them in this case? The young man who had the demon would act like a lunatic, according to his father, so perhaps his bizarre behavior frightened the disciples.

> When Jesus arrived on the scene, the father begged Jesus for help, and He cast out the demon and healed the boy. Then the disciples came to Jesus privately and said, "Why could we not cast it out?" So Jesus said to them, "Because of your unbelief; for assuredly, I say to you, if you have faith as a mustard seed, you will say to this mountain, 'Move from here to there,' and it will move; and nothing will be impossible for you. However,

this kind does not go out except by prayer and fasting." (Matthew 17:19-21)

In defense of the disciples, I will say there was a time in my life when I could not believe God for casting out legions of demons. I would think if it could be done at all, perhaps it could be done over a period of time. But over the last twenty years, my belief system has radically changed. During the Argentine Revival and the Brownsville Revival, I saw men of God cast out multiple demons, and I had to do the same thing myself on many occasions, and God did not let me down. You can walk up to me with eighty-two thousand ugly demons attached to you, and I am going to believe that you are delivered from every single one of them right now and that you will walk away from me free in Christ and in your right mind.

That's what I believe today, and that's what God manifests through my ministry, in part because of my belief.

People think, if I could just see that manifestation, then I would believe! If I could just experience that revival, then my life would be transformed. But Jesus told Thomas, "Thomas, because you have seen Me, you have believed. Blessed are those who have not seen and yet have believed" (John 20:29). Jesus is looking for us to believe it before we see it. He's looking for us to live it before we receive it.

Some people in the Bible tried to convince Jesus that witnessing a miracle would make them accept Him:

> The Pharisees and Sadducees came to Jesus and tested him by asking him to show them a sign from heaven.
>
> He replied, "When evening comes, you say, 'It will be fair weather, for the sky is red,' and in the morning, 'Today it will be stormy, for the sky is red and overcast.' You know how to interpret the appearance of the sky, but you cannot interpret the signs of the times. A wicked and adulterous generation looks for a miraculous sign, but none will be given it except the sign of Jonah." Jesus then left them and went away. (Matthew 16:1-4, NIV)

I find it fascinating that the Pharisees and Sadducees didn't normally hang out together. They disliked each other because there was a struggle between the two groups as to which should be the primary spiritual authority in Israel. But their mutual animosity toward Jesus united them so that they came to Him together to demand a sign. It was almost as if they thought He was a third challenger—an independent— and He might draw votes away from one side or the other!

Jesus recognized that witnessing a sign wouldn't fundamentally change their hearts toward Him, and He told them, in effect: "I have already done miracles and you still don't believe." The same is true for you if you think that witnessing a miracle with your own eyes will give you the faith to live a righteous life. There are plenty of signs all around you that Christ is Lord, and if none of them have inspired you to accept Him and live for Him, then another one isn't going to make any difference. You *know in your heart* there is salvation in no other name. Either you embrace that truth or you don't— witnessing a miracle won't bring about lasting change. Only you can decide.

It's also important to understand that being in the midst of revival or operating in the miraculous does not guarantee righteous behavior. I have been privileged to see legitimate miracles and outpourings of the Spirit of God over the years. Seeing or experiencing miracles may give you a spiritual jolt, but it will not fundamentally change you. Someone could be raised from the dead right in front of you, but if you still have a desire to sin, you are going to go ahead and sin. A mere observance of God's power in action will not build your belief system to the point that you can coast along full of the Spirit and walk in God's ways.

People want to ride the wave of a revival and believe that will keep them on the right path with God, but I have lived right in the middle of two of the biggest revivals of the last hundred years, and I can testify: right in the middle of a move of God, with signs, wonders, and miracles, people can still be as catty, mean, and sinful as at any other time. A move of God will not carry you or sustain you. The excitement of the moment will not keep you from sin. Only an intimate, personal relationship with Jesus Christ will do that.

Another instance of when a miracle did not happen was one we discussed in the previous chapter: Jesus failed to come and heal Lazarus. And in that case, Jesus clearly stated to His disciples, "Lazarus is dead. And I am glad for your sakes that I was not there, that you may believe"

(John 11:14). He had delayed in the manifestation of a miracle specifically to build the belief of the disciples. Then in His prayer at Lazarus's tomb, He told God, "And I know that You always hear Me, but because of the people who are standing by I said this, that they may believe that You sent Me" (John 11:42).

Jesus wanted those at the tomb and those who would hear the story later, even thousands of years later, to believe that Jesus was the Son of God who had God's power to raise the dead.

Belief, simply believing that God has the power to keep His promises to us and will do so, is a *huge* concept for receiving a miracle. It's also a very difficult one for many humans. It was difficult for the disciples and they had lived with Jesus and seen Him perform miracles almost daily. When you look at them after the resurrection, they knew Christ was alive after being dead, and they just went back to fishing. They didn't know what to do. They didn't know how to believe.

What were they doing out there in that boat on the Sea of Tiberius in John 21? They had been with the resurrected Savior, and all they could think to do was revert back to their old ways and go fishing.

That tends to be human nature. We accept Christ as Savior and after a little while we think, "Well, what now? I've had a religious experience." Then we go back to our old ways. But Jesus intends so much more for us! That morning, Jesus found the disciples out in their boat. He came to them, told them where to catch some fish, made them breakfast, and just sat and talked with them. He knew that soon He would ascend to heaven and the disciples would then receive the baptism of the Holy Spirit and that fire from on high would strengthen their belief in Him and turn them into bold evangelists for Him.

He told them, "Wait in Jerusalem a little while. I'll send you the promise of the Father." He didn't tell them what was going to happen to them; He didn't mention the rushing mighty wind or the tongues of fire. He just told them to wait on Him.

If you find your belief wavering as you pray for your miracle, just follow the example of the apostles. Don't go back to your old ways; instead, wait on the Lord and let His Spirit dwell in you to build you in your belief. It may be that God is just waiting on you to trust in Him.

16

REASON #3

C Is for Confidence

THERE ARE TIMES WHEN GOD DOES NOT PERFORM a miracle because He wants our confidence to mature.

Jean Francois Gravelet, the Great Blondin, was the first man ever to walk across Niagara Falls on a tightrope. A showman from the old tradition of European circuses—unhappy ever to repeat a performance—Gravelet went on to walk the tightrope across the falls blindfolded. Once he even stopped in the middle and prepared himself an omelet before passing on to the other side!

Finally he decided he would push a wheelbarrow across the tightrope, and a huge crowd gathered to see if he could do it. The story goes that the Great Blondin brought out the wheelbarrow to excited applause and fanfare. As he prepared to make his crossing, he called out to a man in the crowd, "Do you believe I can cross Niagara Falls on a tightrope pushing this wheelbarrow?"

"Yes, you can do it!" the man enthusiastically cried back.

"Wonderful," said the Great Blondin. "Hop in!"

"Me? No thank you!" was the hasty reply.

It's one thing to know a person is able to do something and quite

Faith is not agitation; it is quiet confidence that God means what He says, and we act on His Word.

—SMITH WIGGLESWORTH (1859-1947)[1]

another to stake your life on what you know. It was one thing for the man to have faith that the Great Blondin could accomplish the amazing feat, but something else altogether for him to entrust himself to the wheelbarrow.

That is the difference between faith and confidence. You can have great faith that Jesus has saved you and that He is with you. But to entrust yourself to His keeping completely requires that you have great confidence in Him too.

Are you confident that Christ will hear and answer your prayers? If not, then it's possible your miracle is just waiting for your confidence to mature.

There are times when God does not perform a miracle because He wants our confidence in Him to mature.

Confidence can also be termed certainty, and I don't want you to think of it as a highly spiritual or religious concept. In fact, I want you to think of it as a very practical and working part of your faith in everyday life. You have confidence that the chair at your office is going to hold your weight, so you sit down in it every day without even thinking about it. You have confidence that the steaks at your favorite restaurant are going to be delicious, so you freely recommend it to others. You have confidence that the roller coaster operators at the amusement park are skilled in their job, so you buckle yourself in and prepare for a great ride. You have confidence that your surgeon is qualified in his profession, so you proceed with the operation.

That is the kind of confidence God wants you to have in Him—that comfortable, reliable, never-a-second-thought confidence that He will be where He said He is going to be and do what He said He is going to do. "Now this is the confidence that we have in Him, that if we ask anything according to His will, He hears us. And if we know that He hears us, whatever we ask, we know that we have the petitions that we have asked of Him" (1 John 5:14-15).

You *can* have complete confidence in Jesus to love you, save you, provide for you, and manifest miracles through you according to His Word. But if you *don't* have that confidence, it's time to work on developing it.

Earlier in this book, we discussed the time Jesus and His disciples were caught in a storm out on a lake. This is one example of how the disciples experienced a lengthy delay of their miracle so that Christ could help them mature in their confidence in Him. It seemed their ship was about to sink, and instead of vigilantly standing watch with them and praying for their survival, Jesus was sleeping through the whole thing!

> On the same day, when evening had come, He said to them, "Let us cross over to the other side." Now when they had left the multitude, they took Him along in the boat as He was. And other little boats were also with Him. And a great windstorm arose, and the waves beat into the boat, so that it was already filling. But He was in the stern, asleep on a pillow. And they awoke Him and said to Him, "Teacher, do You not care that we are perishing?"
>
> Then He arose and rebuked the wind, and said to the sea, "Peace, be still!" And the wind ceased and there was a great calm. But He said to them, "Why are you so fearful? How is it that you have no faith?" And they feared exceedingly, and said to one another, "Who can this be, that even the wind and the sea obey Him!" (Mark 4:35-41)

Now, from our human perspective, you can't much blame the disciples for panicking. Their boat was just about full of water. On the other hand, think of the things the disciples had already seen in their tenure with the Savior, just from Mark's own record:

- The Holy Spirit descended like a dove upon Jesus, and the voice of God declared, "You are my beloved Son" (Mark 1:10-11).
- Jesus cast out an unclean spirit from a man at the synagogue (1:23-27).

- Peter's mother-in-law was healed (1:30-31).
- Jesus healed many people and cast out many demons (1:32-34).
- Jesus preached and cast out demons throughout Galilee (1:39).
- Jesus healed a leper (1:40-42).
- Jesus healed a paralyzed man and read the minds of the Pharisees (2:3-12).
- A deformed hand was healed (3:1-5).
- Jesus healed multitudes and cast out many unclean spirits (3:10-11).

This is quite a résumé of miracles for just the first three chapters of Mark, and it becomes obvious that the disciples had seen Jesus operate in the miraculous a lot. You'd think they would have had confidence in Him to protect them from the storm, but here's that difference between belief and confidence that we talked about: They doubtless believed—had faith—that Jesus had miraculous powers, but when it came to entrusting their lives to those powers, their confidence was low. It was easy to have faith for someone else's healing, but when it came to having confidence that they would not drown on wild, stormy waters in a sinking ship, they came up a little short.

Jesus, asleep on a pillow in the stern, had every confidence that He (and His followers) would be just fine (Mark 4:38). That's why He could sleep.

I am reminded of a friend of mine who had traveled on mission trips in Russia just before and just after the fall of the iron curtain. At that time—and this may have changed since then—the Russian airline Aeroflot, a product of Communism, was something of a national joke.

The flight attendants had been known to be drunk on duty (you could only hope the pilots were sober), and the baggage handlers regularly stole from the suitcases they loaded and unloaded. I remember a flight on Aeroflot when the ceiling of the plane began to fall on the passengers during take off. One man, much to my surprise, stood up in his seat and held the ceiling up as we ascended. My faith was tested that day.

On Aeroflot there seemed to be no limits for carry-on packages, and farmers often boarded with small livestock. The worst of it, of course, was the safety record. Accidents weren't common, but they weren't particularly rare, either.

My friend was directing a video shoot for a missions organization, covering thousands of miles of Russia, Ukraine, and Belarus in one trip that required the proverbial planes, trains, and automobiles. After three days of hurried shooting in a different city each day and three nights of sleeping (or trying to sleep) on rattling Russian trains through Ukraine and Belarus, the director and her American cameraman boarded the four-hour Aeroflot flight for Siberia and almost immediately passed into deep sleep, bone weary, and glad to be able to relax.

When they awakened, their young Russian interpreter, a new believer who appeared to have clung to his seat white knuckled the entire flight, wanted to know, "How could you sleep? Weren't you nervous about flying?"

His words echoed the demands of Jesus's disciples, "Do you not care that we are perishing?" (Mark 4:38). Of course Jesus cared, but He knew they weren't perishing. My friends on the Aeroflot flight didn't have any particular knowledge that their plane wouldn't crash, but what they did have was confidence in Jesus to protect them, come what may. Their Russian interpreter had only been a believer a few months, and Jesus was still maturing that confidence in him.

What kind of storm are you going through? What's buffeting your life? What winds are blowing up against your house? What flood is swamping your boat? Your whole world may be sinking and you are crying out, "Jesus! Wake up! Help me!"

Don't panic. God at times allows our boat to rock and roll; He allows us to get drenched; He allows us to get seasick so that our confidence in Him will be developed through exercising it.

Jesus is in the boat with you, and He will not let you go down. Put your confidence in the Lord. Tell Him, "Lord, I have confidence in You to carry me through, so I am not going to panic. You and I, we're in this together, and I have confidence that You will bring me safely through."

Perhaps Jesus is holding back the miracle answer you need in order to help you develop that inner confidence of knowing that no matter how bad the storm, He has everything under control. Then when the miracle does come, if you have been at the very verge of sinking, imagine the kind of impact it is going to have in your life!

17

REASON #4

D Is for Depth

THERE ARE TIMES WHEN GOD DOES NOT PERFORM a miracle because He may want to test the depth of our passion.

Years ago, I read a quote from Joseph Caryl, a great Puritan writer who said, "According to the weight of the burden that grieves you is the cry to God that comes from you." He was saying, "If something is seriously bothering you, then you will seriously pursue God."

It reminded me of another great Puritan, John Knox, who cried out on his knees to God, "Give me Scotland or I die." He was saying he would withstand anything to see his country saved—prison, beatings, even death. He was saying that his burden to see Scotland saved was greater than his love for life. We all want to see America turn to God, but are any of us crying out with that kind of passion for our nation?

They say that in Africa Christianity is a mile wide and an inch deep. Maybe in America we are two inches deep, but I don't see a lot more depth than that. It seems like there are millions of believers in America who are like those little bonsai trees. They came to Christ, then made a determined effort not to grow another inch, and they stay perfect little baby believers.

There is a certain depth... it is going beyond self to God, to the point where He is first in your life, where you give Him your best, then you ask for His best. That is where your miracle starts. At your depth.

—ORAL ROBERTS[1]

There's no depth to their commitment. It might sound like I am condemning the church, but in fact, I am just telling the truth. When it comes to going after God, too many of us American believers are just wimps.

I have seen men spend more time picking out a set of golf clubs than going after God on their knees. Then they wonder why they can't keep their son off drugs. I've seen women who spend more time on their hair and makeup every morning than in communication with their heavenly Father; then they want to know why God isn't moving in their church.

If you were God, would *you* move in their church, with nobody praying, nobody asking for your help, nobody weeping and travailing for a miracle? I believe in a case like this, the miracle may be delayed or denied because God is looking for people who have a depth of passion, a depth of commitment, a depth of travail for the thing they're seeking.

There are times when God does not perform a miracle simply because He wants to witness the depth of our travail for an answer. We talked about Jonah and his desire to escape God's direction by heading out to sea instead of going to preach in Nineveh. I think after he was tossed into the sea for bringing misfortune to his ship, he started developing a depth of passion very quickly. He was a prophet and God wanted to use him, but at this point—struggling for survival in the deep blue sea and then being swallowed whole by a huge fish—he was actually forced to deepen in his faith even further.

The Scriptures record Jonah's prayer from the belly of the fish:

When my soul fainted within me,
I remembered the LORD;
And my prayer went up to You,
Into Your holy temple.

Those who regard worthless idols
Forsake their own Mercy.
But I will sacrifice to You
With the voice of thanksgiving;
I will pay what I have vowed.
Salvation is of the LORD. (Jonah 2:7-9)

What I love about this prayer is that Jonah got real deep real fast. In the face of certain death, he forgot all about his desire to run away from God's call and instead declared, "I am torn up from the floor up, but I know You can rescue me, God, and there is nothing more important to me right now than serving You." His words, his travail, caused God to look down and in effect say, "Now Jonah's getting it. I think I have finally gotten to the core of my servant Jonah."

Psalm 42:7 says, "Deep calls unto deep at the noise of Your waterfalls; all Your waves and billows have gone over me." I believe that when we develop a depth in our faith commitment, in our love for God and our desire to serve Him, we call out for His deep commitment to us, His deep love for us. When God witnesses a depth of passion and commitment, it calls to His depth of compassion toward us. Deep calls to deep.

God may want to do a great work in your life, but what if there is no depth to your walk to call out to the depth of His love for you? When your prayers are as quick and casual as blessing a bowl of cornflakes, God can see no real commitment in you. You have to go deeper in God to get to the place where He can use you.

I think of the incredible Indian pastor and missionary David Mohan who has taken Madras by storm, launching a church with thousands of believers who can't fit into their building and have bubbled over into hundreds of house-church Bible studies. This great man of God is up at five every morning, and he prays until eight. It's not something he does on special occasions when he needs a real touch from

God; it's something he does every day because he believes the only way to hear from God and experience God is to spend time with God.

There was a woman who needed a miracle in Matthew 15, but she was a Gentile, a Canaanite woman, the Scriptures say. And Jesus had basically restricted His ministry to the Jews because He was their Messiah and the fulfillment of their prophecies. But this Canaanite woman had a daughter who was demon possessed. She needed the Master to save her child.

Think of the great lengths to which a mother will go to protect her baby. She's fierce, and she won't give up. That is the kind of depth of commitment Christ wants us to develop. This woman was no different. She cried out to Jesus for His help, and He didn't even answer her. Did that deter her? No. She followed along after Him, pleading for help, until the disciples asked Jesus to tell her to go away. She was bugging them!

At this point, Jesus turned to her and said, "I was not sent except to the lost sheep of the house of Israel" (Matthew 15:24). He as much as said to her, "I am not going to help you." Did that deter her? No! This was her baby she was trying to save. She couldn't give up. She not only continued to follow Him and cry out to Him, but she went even deeper. She began to worship Jesus in the midst of her need:

> Then she came and worshiped Him, saying, "Lord, help me!" But He answered and said, "It is not good to take the children's bread and throw it to the little dogs." And she said, "Yes, Lord, yet even the little dogs eat the crumbs which fall from their masters' table." (Matthew 15:25-27)

Jesus was floored. He had told her He wasn't going to help her, then He told her that His attention was focused on the Jews, yet she didn't stop asking for His help and worshiping Him. In fact, she had a quick response when He used an analogy to make her see why He couldn't help her. Even the puppies get the crumbs!

She wasn't giving up. She was saying to Him, "Jesus, You can say whatever You want to say. It doesn't matter—insult me, insult my people, whatever. The important thing is that I know You are the Healer. I know You are the Miracle Worker. I know who You are, Lord, and I'm going after You for my daughter because You are the only one who can set her free."

Jesus was impressed with her commitment, with her answer, and with her faith. He healed her daughter. If He knew He was going to do that to begin with, why didn't He respond to her initial cry for help? It wasn't that He didn't hear her. On the contrary, He listened to her every word. He was listening carefully to her heart, probing to the core of her being to see what kind of faith He would find, all the while He was probably thinking, "Look at this woman! She's not going to leave me alone until her daughter is set free."

Jesus was judging her depth. When He was silent, she persisted. When He didn't tell her what she wanted to hear, she worshiped Him. When it looked like the answer would never come, she responded with simple, tenacious faith. Her response, from the depth of her being, touched Jesus in the depth of His being, and she received her miracle.

She was commended for her great faith, and her story was included in our Bible as an example of the depth we need in order to receive a miracle.

My dear friend and mentor, Leonard Ravenhill, has taught me so many lessons about life, ministry, and miracles. I went to him once with a heavy burden about the finances I needed for ministry. I explained my dilemma to him, and I asked him to pray that God would just take this weight off my shoulders.

He said, "There is no way I am going to pray that God would lift this burden from you, and in fact, I have been praying that God would put it on you." I was shocked! Some mentor, praying that I would suffer. Some friend, praying that I would have to struggle. But he went on to say, "Son, if God lifts this burden off you, you won't pray." He knew that when I had no problems to present to God through fervent, daily prayer, I would be tempted not to talk to God at all.

It's the burdens, the problems, the struggles, that develop the depth in us God is looking for. I think of my own mom, Ann Hill, who carried the burden of my sinful life and drug addiction to God every day for years.

One night, about twenty of my buddies and I had just committed a major drug heist. We had made away with hundreds of vials of liquid morphine. This was like Christmas for us druggies! We had taken the stuff to my house and started right in shooting it. We'd pop the vial, plunge in the needle to suck up the morphine, then shoot the narcotics right into our veins. We were just running up morphine as fast as we could.

Because we were boys and because we were idiots, when the needle was empty, we'd flip it up and try to make it stick in the ceiling, like a dart. About midnight, the ceiling of my room was studded with empty syringes, and empty vials littered the floor. Most of the guys were totally passed out, and I was barely awake. The room looked like some kind of junkie hell, like a pile of dead guys all with punctured arms...and that's when my mom walked in.

My mom loved to play Scrabble, and she had been out with her friends for Scrabble night. My room was a basement rec room, so when Mom arrived home, she had to pass from the garage and through my room to get upstairs. She took one look around that horrifying scene and sped up the stairs. Even in my semiconscious state, I still knew that she was going to get on the phone and call the paramedics and the police because we looked like a bunch of corpses down there. If she did that, we'd be busted for the drug heist, possession, and I don't know what all. I had to stop her.

So I went lurching up the stairs, but she wasn't at the phone. I walked through another hallway and saw her bedroom door was closed, so I figured she was calling from her phone in there and my heart just started to pound out of control. If the police showed up, we were all going to be so busted! I slowly opened the door and peeked into her room, prepared to grab the phone out of her hands.

But Mom was on her knees praying, crying out to God, "Jesus, save my son." Rather than calling the police, she called on her hotline to heaven. Kneeling on her little braided rug, she was deep in travail for me. At that moment, I was just so glad she wasn't calling the authorities, I didn't think any more about it. But today, I think about it often.

I think about the angel Gabriel pointing to my mom and saying to Jesus, "She's at it again. Do you hear that?"

I think about the Father, Son, and Spirit saying, "We hear it, and We have a plan for ol' Steve. He's not only going to get saved, but he's going to preach the Gospel all over the world. He's going to be actively involved in great revivals. Her prayer is going to be answered one day soon."

My mom's prayer was answered. Years later, she traveled to several places in the world with me as I held evangelistic crusades. The last meeting she attended was in Finland, where my mom's family is from. She spoke fluent Finnish. And that little Scandinavian country claimed me as their native son and made a big deal out of our being there. The crusade was in a large sports arena and was front-page news. I interviewed my mom on the platform during the services, and she could speak to the crowd in Finnish. They just loved her!

Mom spent years weeping and travailing over me, but when God finally transformed me, she was filled with a joy that lasted the rest of her life. A true prayer warrior, she went after God, and she didn't let Him go. Mom died about a year ago. Great is her reward.

The prayer warriors of Argentina are the same way. My wife, Jeri, and I were part of the great Argentine Revival for nearly eight years where hundreds of thousands of people were saved, healed, and delivered by the power of God. Every night if you looked beneath the platform of the great crusades of Carlos Annacondia, you'd see anywhere from 100 to 150 people on their faces before God, literally roaring out in prayer for the entire service, often lasting five hours.

They didn't pray for five minutes to ask a blessing on the pastor. They prayed for hours every night seeking the face of God from the depths of their being, crying out for souls: "God pour out Your Spirit on Argentina." That's why the revival broke out—that's why countless hundreds of thousands in Argentina know Christ today. Because someone had the depth of a burden for them, and they wouldn't let God go until He blessed them.

Another story that illustrates the importance of having this depth of commitment, burden, passion, and even travail before God is the tale of the cry that made Jesus stand still.

Earlier we discussed the blind man named Bartimaeus of Mark 10. As Jesus was walking with His disciples and a great number of people, He passed by Bartimaeus, who was sitting by the side of the road begging.

Notice that Jesus walked right by him, but when Bartimaeus heard who was passing, he began to cry out to the Savior, "Jesus, Son of David, have mercy on me!" (Mark 10:47). He must have caused quite a disturbance, because all his neighbors told him to shut up.

Jesus continued walking away, but Bartimaeus just yelled louder! In fact, he shouted with such a loud voice, Jesus stopped walking:

> So Jesus stood still and commanded him to be called.
>
> Then they called the blind man, saying to him, "Be of good cheer. Rise, He is calling you."
>
> And throwing aside his garment, he rose and came to Jesus. So Jesus answered and said to him, "What do you want Me to do for you?"
>
> The blind man said to Him, "Rabboni, that I may receive my sight."
>
> Then Jesus said to him, "Go your way; your faith has made you well." And immediately he received his sight and followed Jesus on the road. (Mark 10:49-52)

What made Jesus stop in His tracks that day? What was He looking for? I am so convinced that He was looking for the deep, profound craving for Him that Bartimaeus displayed. The crowds were following Jesus because they heard He had fed the five thousand and could do miracles. He was a mysterious man performing marvelous wonders. But Bartimaeus went after Him for a specific thing that he needed—healing—and he refused to shut up or forget about it when others discouraged him. Deep calls to deep. The depth of his need spoke to the depth of Christ's love.

Now if you are in bed with a terminal illness and don't have the strength to pick up a spoon, I am not advising you to get on your face before God and travail for hours. But maybe there are friends and neighbors who can call on God for you. He wants to see how deep you will go to pursue what you need from Him.

I believe this is what God liked about Jacob. He was extreme. He just wouldn't give up, no matter what obstacles came his way.

When Jacob disguised himself and tricked his father to inherit his brother's blessing, he went about it the wrong way. But the fact that he went to such an extreme to inherit a spiritual blessing caught God's attention. And he received the blessing.

He worked tirelessly for fourteen years to gain Rachel's hand in marriage. Genesis 29:19 tells us that the years seemed like only a few days to Jacob because of his love for Rachel. How many men do you think would work for fourteen years simply to earn a lady's hand in marriage?

One night God came to Jacob in the form of a man, and they wrestled all night: "And He said, 'Let Me go, for the day breaks.' But he said, 'I will not let You go unless You bless me!' So He said to him, 'What is your name?' He said, 'Jacob.' And He said, 'Your name shall no longer be called Jacob, but Israel; for you have struggled with God and with men, and have prevailed'" (Genesis 32:26-28). Because of his wrestling, he obtained a spiritual blessing that changed his whole life.

My friend, there are times when you need to hold on to God like that and wrestle to receive your miracle. If you are still waiting for your miracle, don't give up! If you can hold on to God through the dark night of struggle, it may be that deep will call to deep—the depth of your travail will speak to the depth of God's love and bring about your miracle. If you give up now, you might just miss out. Hold on...and maybe go a little deeper!

18

REASON #5

E Is for Energy

THERE ARE TIMES WHEN GOD DOES NOT PERFORM a miracle because He may want us to invest more energy.

Have you ever found yourself slumped in your La-Z-Boy, mindlessly staring at the TV, hating what's on? You want to change the channel, but there's a problem. The remote is on the arm of the couch...several feet away! You know a decision must be made. To watch what you want will require an exertion of energy. You must rouse yourself from the chair and drag yourself across the room to reach that desired object. How is it that such a simple, low-energy task can be stretched out and delayed for such a miserable span of time? There are times when it is much easier just to sit back and stare at whatever is on the screen. This may seem trivial or silly, but it reminds me of the lack of energy that we find in Christian circles today.

If you think about it, that's the way some believers behave when they are praying for a miracle. Let's say Chrissy Christian has been praying for worldwide revival for ten years. Every day, she prays, "And God, send a revival! I really want to see my whole neighborhood saved! I want to see everyone in my city saved."

You must not think that these gifts will fall upon you like ripe cherries. There is a sense in which you have to pay the price for everything you get. We must be covetous for God's best gifts, and say Amen to any preparation the Lord takes us through.

—SMITH WIGGLESWORTH (1859-1947)[1]

It's a great prayer, and if Chrissy is praying it like those Argentinean prayer warriors I told you about in the previous chapter, then I believe God is certainly hearing her prayers and wants to respond. But, if Chrissy really has a heart to see her neighborhood saved, she could do even more than pray, couldn't she?

If she never invited a single neighbor to come to church with her, she hasn't invested much in winning her neighborhood to Jesus. If she never took the time to have a Bible study in her home, then she hasn't tried hard to win her city. Prayer is a big part of a miracle, but God may ask you to expend some energy, too.

If you haven't experienced your miracle yet and you know it is in line with God's Word; if you have travailed in prayer over it and you have confidence and belief that God can and will answer your prayer; then maybe the reason you haven't received it yet is that God is waiting for you to get up out of the La-Z-Boy and expend some energy.

There are times when God does not perform a miracle because His people are unwilling to put forth the energy to bring it to pass. This energy is closely related to the depth we discussed in the previous chapter, but they are not exactly the same. There is more to investing your energy than simply investing the depth of your soul and passion.

In Mark 2, we read about the four friends who wanted to get their paralyzed friend to Jesus. The house was so crowded they couldn't get in to see the Savior, but they didn't let that deter them. They hauled that poor man on his cot up to the roof, tore up the roof tiles, and lowered the sick man down by ropes. That's more than just a depth of belief; that is getting down and expending some elbow grease to make the miracle happen. That's energy!

Or think about the woman with the issue of blood in Mark 5. She had been bleeding for twelve years. I know it's not fun to think about, but here's the fact: If you are losing blood all the time, you get anemic, and anemia makes you weak and tired. After twelve years of it, that poor lady was probably white as a sheet, thin as a rail, and completely worn out. She had nothing left. But she heard about Jesus, and she thought to herself, "If I can just touch the hem of His clothes, I'll be made whole."

So this tired, sick, weak woman not only got herself together to go out into the city, but she pushed through a crowd of people to get close to the Master. People were thick around Jesus. When He felt the healing power go out from Him and stopped to ask, "Who touched Me?" the disciples thought He was crazy—everyone was touching Him! They were packed together like sardines, and He was asking who touched Him? Yet somehow in the crush of that throng, a little sick woman managed to elbow her way to the front and touch Jesus's clothes.

She didn't *have* any energy, but she pulled it up from somewhere and spent it all to come to Christ. Sometimes to get your miracle, God expects you to make some kind of effort.

I think of a woman named Vickie who goes to our church. She had suffered clinical depression for nearly six years, and nothing seemed to help her. She was in such bondage to hopelessness, fear, and despair, sometimes the only place she felt safe was in the corner of her closet or even under her bed. The fear and desolation she felt kept her from leaving the house except in extreme emergencies, and then she was terrified until she could get back home. The disease had all but crippled her.

Then she heard that we would be launching Heartland Fellowship. She knew that I had been part of the Brownsville Revival, and she had heard that miracles happened there. So she made a commitment to herself that somehow she would come to church. I don't know how someone who is terrified of walking through the front door of her house found the strength and courage to come across town to a crowded church, but she was there the very first Sunday. And God met her there!

She told me the music, worship, and preaching all felt like a cool breeze blowing over her. All the fear and depression vanished while Vickie basked in the presence of God. And each time she would return for another service, she received another healing touch from God. Soon her whole life began to change! She found she could leave the house without fear, shop at the grocery store, and do the normal things you and I take for granted!

A year ago, she was cowering in the corner of her closet, full of anxiety for reasons she could not fathom. Today, she is actively involved in the church, sings in the choir, and has already gone on her first missions trip. Her life has been transformed, and it all began with her determination to fight her fears, expend her energy, and come to the place where she knew God would be.

Your heavenly Father doesn't expect you to make an effort to heal yourself or make the impossible happen. That's His area because He is God, and only He can do that. But He might expect you to expend energy in some other fashion, like Vickie did. The Bible gives some clear commands about ways we should expend our energy when we are searching for God's answers (emphasis is mine):

- "**Praise** the LORD! Oh, give thanks to the LORD, for He is good! For His mercy endures forever" (Psalm 106:1).
- "**Seek** the LORD while He may be found" (Isaiah 55:6a).
- "**Call upon** Him while He is near" (Isaiah 55:6b).
- "**Ask**, and it will be given to you; **seek**, and you will find; **knock**, and it will be opened to you" (Matthew 7:7).
- "**Let your light so shine** before men, that they may see your good works and glorify your Father in heaven" (Matthew 5:16).
- "The night is far spent, the day is at hand. Therefore let us cast off the works of darkness, and let us **put on the armor** of light" (Romans 13:12).
- "Therefore, my beloved, as you have always obeyed, not as in my presence only, but now much more in my absence, **work** out your own salvation with fear and trembling" (Philippians 2:12).

- "Finally, brethren, whatever things are true, whatever things are noble, whatever things are just, whatever things are pure, whatever things are lovely, whatever things are of good report, if there is any virtue and if there is anything praiseworthy—**meditate** on these things" (Philippians 4:8).
- "Let the word of Christ dwell in you richly in all wisdom, **teaching** and **admonishing** one another in psalms and hymns and spiritual songs, **singing** with grace in your hearts to the Lord" (Colossians 3:16).
- "Let us therefore **come boldly** to the throne of grace, that we may obtain mercy and find grace to help in time of need" (Hebrews 4:16).

We can ask, seek, and knock; we can praise and pray; we can come boldly; we can teach, admonish, meditate, sing—we can do all kinds of things to seek God's face and pursue His miracle response. We can use our energy for Him.

Self-effort is condemned. You can never *make* a miracle happen. Jesus Himself, the Miracle Maker and Son of the Miracle Maker, said that He could do nothing apart from the Father. The Bible makes it very clear, and the entire book of Galatians speaks specifically to the truth that our salvation is the gift of God and that we can do nothing to add to it. Rather, we must let Jesus live through us. Galatians 2:20 says, "I have been crucified with Christ; it is no longer I who live, but Christ lives in me; and the life which I now live in the flesh I live by faith in the Son of God, who loved me and gave Himself for me."

In Jesus, we are complete. His work on the cross was perfect. There is nothing we can add to it. There is no doubt of that, and what I am telling you here about expending your energy cannot supersede or add anything to what Jesus has done for you. I don't want you to think that I am saying some work of yours will bring a miracle to being, because it won't. Only God can supernaturally bring about a miracle.

What I am saying is that God has every right to ask you to get involved in the miracle for which you are praying and believing, in whatever fashion.

A popular scripture today among those who are praying for revival in the U.S.A. is 2 Chronicles 7:14: "If My people who are called by My name will humble themselves, and pray and seek My face, and turn from their wicked ways, then I will hear from heaven, and will forgive their sin and heal their land."

Take a close look at this and you will see that getting God's blessing requires expending no small amount of energy. We have to humble ourselves and pray, seek God's face, turn from our wicked ways—energy, energy, energy. In fact, the part of that verse that takes the most energy may be "turn from their wicked ways." Nobody likes to preach on that—we preach on the "humble ourselves, pray, and seek God's face" part—but it takes a lot of energy to turn from our bad habits: to say no to drugs and alcohol if we've been addicted, to say no to the girl at the office who's treating you a lot nicer than your wife is, to say no to the chance to save a bundle on taxes by cooking the books just a little.

People want God to do a miracle for them, but they don't want to put any of their own energy into the project. I am so thankful for the man who poured his energy into telling my wife, Jeri, about Jesus. She didn't make it easy, and he had to do more than just pray for her.

My wife grew up with a loving mom, but a violent, alcoholic stepfather. She was unhappy at home and drifted into drugs as a teenager and then deep into a party lifestyle. Eventually she was arrested for dealing drugs. She has told me, at that point, she hated life and did not believe there was any hope in the future for her. She thought drugs, alcohol, and—if she weren't careful—jail time were all she had to look forward to.

One Saturday morning, the local pastor knocked on the door of her parents' home. Someone had told him about Jeri, and he felt a real burden for her soul. When she answered, he introduced himself and told her that Jesus loved her.

It was the last thing Jeri wanted to hear. She didn't believe anybody loved her! She became indignant, told the pastor she wasn't interested, and closed the door in his face.

The very next Saturday, he came back and told her, "Jeri, Jesus loves you, and He has a plan for your life." This time she was even more blunt with him and slammed the door.

The next Saturday he came back, and this time Jeri's stepfather answered the door. He shouted at the preacher, "If you come back to this house one more time, I'll have you arrested for trespassing!"

The next Saturday, he was back. He came back almost every Saturday for two years. Every visit ended the same way—with someone slamming the door in his face.

He had discovered that most drug addicts can be found at home between 8:00 a.m. and noon—they party all night, and by the light of day they drag home, hung over. So that is the time he would visit each week.

It took a lot of energy for him to keep coming back, but you ain't seen nothing yet. One Saturday morning in October 1975, the pastor showed up at his usual time, and no one came to the door. He hammered on it for a while, thinking he would wake Jeri from a stupor—but still no answer. The house was completely empty. The family had moved.

This was the perfect opportunity for him to give up. After all, he had expended two years of time and energy on Jeri for no return, but he didn't give up. Instead, he went home and cried out to God, "Lord, I've been faithful to share Your love with this girl for the last two years. You see what's happened, and since You are omnipresent, I have just one question for you. Where is she now?!"

The Lord answered with a vision. The pastor saw a white house and the number of a highway. That was good enough for him. He raced from intercession to intersection. Turning down the highway, he began to scan the sides of the road for the house in his vision. He had no idea where he was going, but God had it all planned out. Jeri was home alone.

He spotted the house, turned into the driveway, slipped out of his car as he had done every Saturday for the last two years, walked up the steps as he murmured a prayer, and knocked on the door. When Jeri answered, her jaw dropped, and she said, "How did you find me?"

Without missing a beat, the pastor said, "Jeri, Jesus told me where you were because He loves you and has a plan for your life."

Mystified, Jeri opened her door and said, "Come on in." The pastor prayed with her that very day. A few days later, she went to Teen Challenge, the faith-based drug rehab ministry, and became an on-fire Christian. A year and a half later we met, were soon married, and have just celebrated twenty-five years of marital bliss. Thank God that pastor didn't give up on Jeri. Thank God he was willing to invest his time and energy to show her that Jesus loved her.

Jesus did all the work of salvation when He went to the cross for us, but even today He asks us to invest our time and energy in sharing that good news. Revival doesn't just happen. People who accomplish great things for God don't do so by accident. Churches that bring multitudes to Christ don't do so by just dreaming about it.

Great things happen through God's grace and the willingness of His people to invest their strength, their time, their energy, their very lives into the kingdom.

Are you waiting for an answer from God or a miracle? Perhaps *He* is waiting on *you* to put forth the energy to make it happen.

19

Reason #6

F Is for Failure… It's Not What You Think!

SOME REQUESTS FOR MIRACLES SEEM DELAYED OR DENIED because of our failure to recognize the miracle when it comes.

Have you ever been snorkeling or scuba diving? As I've already mentioned, I'm a scuba diver. I love exploring the wonders of God's underwater world. I also love getting back on the boat after a dive and hearing from all the divers what they saw and experienced, and, especially, discussing with my dive buddy exactly what we saw down there. Half the fun of the dive is being able to share with others about it. Every once in a while I hear some crazy stuff on the boat about what they saw:

"What were you pointing at down by that big coral head? I was trying to photograph that lobster!"

"There was a big flat fish with fins coming off the top and bottom, right next to you with all bright colors and big horse eyes. I wanted you to take a picture of that fish. It was cool."

"Well what was it? Was it an angelfish? They're flat. Was it a rock beauty? That's yellow and black. But there's lots of them, and you totally ruined my chance to get a picture of the lobster."

"I *know* what an angel fish and a rock beauty are, and it wasn't that.

It was shaped more like a diamond, and it had things around its eyes like eyeliner, and it was big. It was practically right in your face. I don't know how you missed it."

"A trigger fish? They're kind of diamond shaped. But the one with eyeliner is a queen trigger fish—was it yellow and blue and green and black? That's a queen trigger fish, but they never come near divers. They're too shy."

"Give me that fish ID chart, and I'll show you what it was. It was right next to you like it was posing for a picture, and you missed it! Well, no, it was shaped like this one, but colored like that and…"

Maybe there was a queen trigger fish and the guy with the camera didn't see it. He's right, they are shy, and it's tricky to get a good photo of one. But maybe it was just an angel fish or a parrot fish, which are common in many places. The problem is, pretty as it was and near as it was, no one recognized it for what it was (whatever it was).

Much of what we have been praying and begging God for, He has already given us, and it has only been awaiting our action.

—T. L. Osborn[1]

Sometimes that is the case when we are asking God to make a move in our lives. He has already made His move, and we just don't recognize it for what it is.

Sometimes requests for miracles seem discarded or delayed because of *our* failure to recognize the miracle when it comes.

You may wonder how that could happen. I mean, if your body needs healing, you'll know when the healing manifests. Right? Or if you need finances, you'll know when the money is in your checking account. Right? If a relationship needs to be restored, surely you'll know when there's peace and harmony in your home. So how could you fail to recognize your miracle when it comes?

Sometimes this happens because we have a specific mindset of how God is going to bring this miracle about. This happened to many of the children of Israel when their Messiah came two thousand years ago. Their idea for a Savior was a conquering King who would make the occupying empire of Rome a footstool for their feet. They were expecting all the glory and splendor described in the Scriptures for the *second* coming of Christ, not realizing that first the Lamb of God had to die for their sins.

When Jesus, the Man of Sorrows, came they did not recognize Him:

For He shall grow up before Him as a tender plant,
And as a root out of dry ground.
He has no form or comeliness;
And when we see Him,
There is no beauty that we should desire Him.
He is despised and rejected by men,
A Man of sorrows and acquainted with grief.
And we hid, as it were, our faces from Him;
He was despised, and we did not esteem Him.

Surely He has borne our griefs
And carried our sorrows;
Yet we esteemed Him stricken,
Smitten by God, and afflicted. (Isaiah 53:2-4)

Little did the Pharisees know when they orchestrated the death of the Savior, they were helping Him to fulfill centuries of messianic prophecy. They simply could not recognize the Messiah when He came, because they expected Him in a different form. What a tragedy for countless millions around the world who do not recognize the Savior.

Think of the Muslim world, from the Middle East and North Africa to the Philippines and Indonesia—millions of Muslims recognize Issa, the Muslim name of Jesus, as a historical figure, a prophet, someone whose words appear in their own Koran. But because they look to the teachings of Mohammed for their salvation, they do not recognize that only Jesus can give them eternal life.

But I want to tell you something about that. There is a miracle move of God going on right now in Muslim communities. I have heard of an entire African village of Muslims turning to Christ, not because of missionaries or crusades, but because a stunning man in radiant white appeared in a dream to one or more of the villagers and explained that only Jesus Christ is the way to salvation. Jesus interrupts our preconceived notions to save us, and as mentioned before, every miracle is somehow about souls.

In the past fifteen years, more Muslims have come to Christ than ever before. For more than ten years, Muslims have been reporting these dream appearances of Jesus. One survey of 600 Muslims who had accepted Christ as Savior showed that fully 25 percent of them came to Jesus because He appeared to them in a dream! Do you know *any* Americans who came to Christ because of a dream? Isn't it awesome that where missionaries can't go, Jesus Himself is going?!

That's a miracle in itself! You and I have been praying for a way to reach the Muslim world with the good news of Jesus, and already Issa Himself is delivering the message of salvation via dreams and visions. Amen!

There is another instance in the Bible where the miracle had happened, but it took a long while for the believers to recognize it. In Acts 12, remember, Peter had been imprisoned by Herod, who planned to have him executed in order to please the religious authorities of the day. Faithful Christians prayed and interceded continually on Peter's behalf. Herod had already murdered James; the believers did not want to lose Peter, too. They were desperate, and in their desperation they cried out to God night and day.

One night while they prayed for Peter, God sent an angel to break Peter out of jail! Of course, the believers were unaware that Peter had been set free. Then there was a knock on the door at the prayer meeting:

> And as Peter knocked at the door of the gate, a girl named Rhoda came to answer. When she recognized Peter's voice, because of her gladness she did not open the gate, but ran in and announced that Peter stood before the gate. But they said to her, "You are beside yourself!" Yet she kept insisting that it was so. So they said, "It is his angel."

Now Peter continued knocking; and when they opened the door and saw him, they were astonished. But motioning to them with his hand to keep silent, he declared to them how the Lord had brought him out of the prison. (Acts 12:13-17)

This scene is one of the most hilarious in the Bible—God must have put it in there to make us chuckle. Here they were praying for Peter to be delivered, and when he was, they didn't believe it. First they thought Rhoda was imagining things, and then they thought Peter had been murdered and it was his spirit at the door. Their miracle had happened, and they did not even recognize it.

At other times a miracle is happening, but for some reason we are willing to settle for much less than what God intends for us. In Mark we learn about a blind man who came to Jesus for healing:

So He took the blind man by the hand and led him out of the town. And when He had spit on his eyes and put His hands on him, He asked him if he saw anything. And he looked up and said, "I see men like trees, walking." Then He put His hands on his eyes again and made him look up. And he was restored and saw everyone clearly. (Mark 8:23-25)

Midway through the miracle, Jesus stopped and asked the blind man, "How's that working for you?" Considering the man was totally blind to begin with, he could have been thrilled to be able to see anything, even if it were a little blurry. He could have said, "That's great, Jesus! I can see—thank You!" and gone on his way, at least functional.

But he wasn't content with a partial miracle. He told Christ the truth, "Uh, not so good." And Jesus completely restored him to perfect vision. I preached a message on this portion of Scripture entitled "The Levels of Life." The *lower level life* is the place of blindness. We all, at one time in our lives, have been there. The *middle level life* is when we receive a touch from Jesus. Sadly, this is where most Christians live. They have had a religious experience but have not entered in to what God has for them. The *upper level life* is where God wants us to live. Jesus wants us *all* to enjoy perfect spiritual vision.

You don't have to settle for partial blindness, either. I see this in the lives of some of the drug addicts who come to Heartland Fellowship and get delivered from their drug addiction, but then they still have the nasty habit of smoking cigarettes. How can they believe God to set them free from the bondage of something as powerfully addictive as crack cocaine but not have the faith that He can set them free from tobacco? They've settled for a partial miracle. They don't recognize that God has already given them the miracle of complete freedom.

I don't care for the partial miracle. If somebody comes to me and asks me to pray for their body to be healed, I don't want to see them walking away from me with a limp. I want to see them walking and leaping and praising God. Somebody will say, "Now, that's a whole lot better!" But I don't want a whole lot better—I want 100 percent whole.

So be on the lookout for your miracle. It might come in a different form from what you expect—be sure you recognize it. You might be tempted to settle for less than what God has in store for you—be sure you claim your *whole* miracle.

On Calvary, Jesus was not alone. Remember the two thieves who were crucified with Him? They were being executed for their crimes, only moments from death. It seems an unlikely place for a miracle, doesn't it? But if you remember, one of those men did recognize his miracle when it appeared:

> Then one of the criminals who were hanged blasphemed Him, saying, "If You are the Christ, save Yourself and us."
>
> But the other, answering, rebuked him, saying, "Do you not even fear God, seeing you are under the same condemnation? And we indeed justly, for we receive the due reward of our deeds; but this Man has done nothing wrong." Then he said to Jesus, "Lord, remember me when You come into Your kingdom."
>
> And Jesus said to him, "Assuredly, I say to you, today you will be with Me in Paradise." (Luke 23:39-43)

Both thieves were witnessing the miracle of salvation as it unfolded. They were in the presence of the "the Lamb slain from the foundation of the world" (Revelation 13:8). Both were about to slip into either eternal separation from God or eternal joy in God's kingdom. One recognized the hand of God extended to save him; the other didn't. It can be just that easy to miss your miracle.

So keep your eyes open. Your miracle could be here any moment now, and I want you to recognize it.

CONCLUSION

Believing God for the Miraculous

I TOLD YOU WHEN WE STARTED THIS JOURNEY together that God *wants* to perform miracles—to save our loved ones, heal our bodies, prosper us, and answer our prayers. The Word of God clearly shows us that He wants to use *every* believer to heal the sick, cast out devils, and manifest His power.

I believe that as you practice the keys I've given you in this book, you will begin to operate in the miraculous, and I hope you will let me know how God is using you!

But if you are not experiencing miracles right now, I want you to take heart, because I believe your miracles are on the way. Look at Gideon in Judges 6. His people were oppressed by the Midianites who would swoop down and carry off all their livestock and crops, leaving Israel starving. Gideon was so afraid of the marauders, he was threshing wheat in the winepress to try to hide from them.

Then an angel appeared to him, calling him a mighty man of valor, and declared that the Lord was with him! Here's Gideon's response:

O my lord, if the LORD is with us, why then has all this happened to us? And *where are all His miracles* which our fathers

Time, which is more precious than rubies or diamonds, is slipping by, and your opportunity will soon be gone. Look at that poor wretch groveling in the mire of sin: he needs to be told of the power of God to save. Look at that dear saint agonizing in the languishing bed of sickness; she needs to hear of the power of God to heal.

—GEORGE JEFFREYS
(1892-1962)[1]

told us about, saying, "Did not the LORD bring us up from Egypt?" But now the LORD has forsaken us and delivered us into the hands of the Midianites. (Judges 6:13, italics added)

In essence, Gideon was saying, "Sure, other people received miracles. Our fore-fathers had their share of the miraculous. But where's *my* miracle?"

If that's how you feel right now after reading about all the fabulous miracles of the Bible and miracles that are happening even right now, today, that's good. It wasn't but a few days after Gideon asked that question—where's my miracle?—that God used him to utterly destroy his enemies and rescue Israel. Your miracle could be that close at hand.

But even if it isn't, you can still trust God to walk you through the circumstances. Look at Shadrach, Meshach, and Abed-Nego in Daniel 3. When they refused to worship the Babylonian king's golden statue, they were sentenced to be thrown alive into a fiery fur-nace. When the king asked if they really thought their God would deliver them from that certain death, they answered:

We have no need to answer you in this matter. If that is the case, our God whom we serve is able to deliver us from the burning fiery furnace, and He will deliver us from your hand, O king. But if not, let it be known to you, O king, that we do not serve your gods, nor will we worship the gold image which you have set up. (Daniel 3:16-18)

They were saying, "If God delivers us, that is good, but even if He chooses not to, we won't worship your idol."

God may choose not to act in the fashion you want Him to or in the timing you want Him to. The important thing is for you to put your trust and confidence in Him. If you've been reading this book while praying for your own miracle healing and you aren't healed yet, that's okay. "There is therefore now no condemnation to those who are in Christ Jesus, who do not walk according to the flesh, but according to the Spirit" (Romans 8:1).

Whether you receive healing or not is not necessarily a reflection on you or the state of your faith. Consider what I've been saying. You must see your healing coming in God's timing, And if it doesn't come on this earth, if you are a child of the King, you know that in heaven you will have complete and perfect everlasting health.

The bottom line on miracles is that every believer has already received the ultimate miracle. We have gone from helpless, hopeless people doomed to eternity in hell without Christ to victorious, faith-filled people destined for glory with God forever:

For if the word spoken through angels proved steadfast, and every transgression and disobedience received a just reward, how shall we escape if we neglect so great a salvation, which at the first began to be spoken by the Lord, and was confirmed to us by those who heard Him, God also bearing witness both with signs and wonders, with various miracles, and gifts of the Holy Spirit, according to His own will? (Hebrews 2:2-4)

Our miracle is always found in the Person of our Lord Jesus Christ, who provided for us "so great a salvation" through His own death and resurrection. In Him dwells every good and perfect gift, and He is the source for every miracle, every breakthrough, and every answer that you will ever need.

You may not see your miracle today. That's okay, too.

Did you ever hear the story of a missionary named Jim Elliot in the 1950s who was called to reach a fierce tribe of Indians in Ecuador known as the Huaorani? That word means "people" in their language, but their neighboring tribes called them the Aucas, which means "savages." The other Indian tribes feared the Aucas because they were so bloodthirsty. For centuries, they had killed all strangers. Recently they had killed several employees of the Shell Oil company.

But Jim Elliot found it unfair that many people around the world hear the Gospel story many times, while this isolated tribe had never heard it once because no one could get close enough to them. He followed God's call and joined a missionary team of men to approach the Aucas. It was his prayer to win that tribe to Jesus.

In January of 1956, Jim and a missionary team, including Christian pilot Nate Saint, Ed McCully, Peter Fleming, and Roger Youderian, first approached the village. They had been flying over and leaving gifts for the tribe for months and had even learned enough of their language to communicate friendly messages. They felt the time for a meeting was right.

But they had also been warned about the Auca savagery, so they decided to carry guns. This was the agreement: if attacked, they would shoot into the air in hopes of frightening the attackers, but they would not shoot *at* anyone, not even to save their own lives. Two days after their initial contact with the Aucas, the attack came. The missionaries fired their pistols into the air, but it didn't stop the Auca warriors, and all five missionaries were slain.

All of Jim Elliot's hopes and dreams of winning this tribe to Jesus were dashed. No miracle saved his life, and no miracle seemed likely to bring such hostile people to repentance through Jesus. Although he had asked in faith believing for the Aucas, Elliot's mission was a terrible failure.

Or was it?

Less than three years later, Nate Saint's sister Rachel and Jim Elliot's widow, Elisabeth, returned to the Auca settlement. They moved in. Jim Elliot's children grew up in the village. Rachel and Elisabeth shared the Gospel, provided healthcare, and began developing a written form of the language. They found the Aucas amazingly open to Jesus. Soon, the majority of the tribe members had come to Christ!

Why? Much later, one of the Aucas who had been party to slaying the missionaries said that for centuries they regarded all strangers as dangerous, because almost every contact with outsiders had resulted in one side attempting to kill the other. They regarded the missionary team no differently when they arrived.

When the warriors attacked and saw that the men were armed, they knew they had been correct! They thought these men had come to kill them.

But then none of the missionaries shot at a single Auca, even as the tribesmen ran them through with spears. They chose to die without lifting a hand to defend themselves, rather than to harm any of the people on their mission field.

At that point the Aucas realized too late that the missionaries would have been their friends, would have died for them, indeed, *had* died, rather than take any of their lives.

When Rachel and Elisabeth explained to the Aucas the Gospel story, they understood innately the sacrifice of Jesus, who laid down His life to spare them from eternal death.

Jim Elliot's dream came true. His miracle happened but in a way he had not planned and after he was dead and gone. But the manner of his death was the catalyst for opening the people's hearts to Jesus on his mission field.

So don't despair. Your miracle may come tomorrow, or it may come after you've gone home to heaven like Jim Elliot's did.

I encourage you today to let the truths of this message and the message of this whole book penetrate your heart and cause you to press on and believe God for the miraculous in your life and the lives of others.

As God begins to bring people across your path who have big needs, don't think for a moment that it is an accident. Be willing and available for God to use you to touch them. Then watch what He will do in and through you.

Yes, you, too, can operate in the miraculous!

Notes

Introduction
1. Lester Sumrall, *The Gifts and Ministries of the Holy Spirit* (South Bend, IN: Sumrall Publishing, 1996), 18.

Chapter 1
1. John G. Lake, *John G. Lake: His Life, His Sermons, His Boldness of Faith* (Fort Worth, TX: Kenneth Copeland Publications, 1994), 532.

Section 1 Introduction
1. Quote about Reinhard Bonnke by Colin Whittaker, *A Passion for the Gospel* (East Sussex, England: Kingsway Publications, 1998), 94.

Chapter 3
1. Quote about Reinhard Bonnke by Whittaker, *Passion for the Gospel*, 107.

Chapter 4
1. Kathryn Kuhlman, *God Can Do It Again* (Englewood Cliffs, NJ: Prentice-Hall, 1969), 23.

Chapter 5
1. Carlos Annacondia, Videos: Argentine Revival, www.fireonthealtar.com/video.

Chapter 6
1. Derek Prince, *The Spirit-Filled Believer's Handbook* (Lake Mary, FL: Creation House, 1993), 486.

Chapter 7
1. F. W. Robertson, as quoted in R. A. Bertran, *The Homiletic Encyclopedia* (New York: Funk & Wagnall's, 1889), 596.

Section 2 Introduction
1. Lake, *Lake: His Life, His Sermons, His Boldness of Faith*, 288.

Chapter 9
1. Prince, *Spirit-Filled Believer's Handbook*, 348–49.

Chapter 10
1. Kathryn Kuhlman, *I Believe In Miracles* (Englewood Cliffs, NJ: Prentice-Hall, 1962), 198

Chapter 11
1. Jonathan Edwards, *The Surprising Work of God* (Boston, MA: James Loring. 1831), 83.

Chapter 12
1. T. L. Osborn, *Healing the Sick* (Tulsa, OK: Harrison House, 1959), 380–82.

Chapter 13
1. Smith Wigglesworth, as quoted in Roberts Liardon, comp., *Smith Wigglesworth: The Complete Collection of His Life Teachings* (Tulsa OK: Albury Publishing, 1996), 473.

Chapter 14
1. F. B. Meyer, *Elijah and the Secret of His Power* (Fort Washington, PA: Christian Literature Crusade, 1960), 184.

Chapter 15
1. Prince, *Spirit-Filled Believer's Handbook*, 332–33.

Chapter 16
1. Smith Wigglesworth, as quoted in W. Hacking, *Smith Wigglesworth Remembered* (Tulsa, OK: Harrison House, 1981), 102.

Chapter 17
1. Oral Roberts, *Miracle of Seed Faith* (Grand Rapids, MI: Revell: 1970), 40–41.

Chapter 18
1. Smith Wigglesworth, as quoted in Liardon, *Smith Wigglesworth,*
347–48.

Chapter 19
1. T. L Osborn, *Faith's Testimony* (Tulsa, OK: Osborn Foundation,
1973), 65.

Conclusion
1. George Jeffreys, as quoted in Ernest C. W. Boulton, *A Ministry of the
Miraculous* (London: Elim Publishing, n.d.), 140.